PRAISE FOR *IN THIS TOGETHER*

"Whether our problem is isolation in a male-dominant culture, distance across racial barriers, living in front of a computer screen, or all three, Nancy O'Reilly's *In This Together* will help us to create community, success, and well-being."

—**Gloria Steinem**, feminist activist and organizer

"Through rigorous research interviews, insight, and analysis, Dr. Nancy D. O'Reilly has produced delightfully informative required reading for women—and men— in all career phases and industries. We all need *In This Together: How Successful Women Support Each Other in Work and Life* to understand and navigate our own power, abundance, strengths, excellence, bias, and generosity to be who we dream we can be."

—**Michele Weldon**, author, journalist, emerita faculty at Northwestern University, and editorial director of Take The Lead

"I grew up hearing that girls didn't do this and girls didn't do that, and did not have a female mentor until I was fifty-five. Dr. Nancy O'Reilly shares many strategies to help women rewind those old tapes and create new ones. I found myself on so many of the pages. As an advocate for women, I know that being *for* women does not mean we are *against* men. Dr. O'Reilly creates the perfect scenarios for women and men to work together. This is the newest tool in my toolbox."

—**Judy Hoberman**, president of Walking on the Glass Floor and Selling In A Skirt

"From the boardroom to the home front, this book tells us how to take charge and lead the way with our innate qualities of communication, collaboration, courage, and perseverance. In this well-researched must-read, Nancy O'Reilly motivates us to come together for the future of womankind and all humanity, offers real strategies and personal stories from women who are making it happen, and compels us to be a part of this powerful time in history. We can do this!"

—**Linda Rendleman**, MS, president of the Women Like Us Foundation

"Every young woman who hasn't stepped into her power yet, every woman in a leadership role, and every man who's confused about what his role should be needs to read *In This Together*. Dr. O'Reilly's new insights, inspiration, practical advice, and innovative solutions give us a pathway to achieving gender equality. Finally."

—**Cheryl Benton**, founder and publisher of *The Three Tomatoes*, coauthor of *Leading Women*, and author of *Can You See Us Now?*

PRAISE FOR *IN THIS TOGETHER*

"Dr. Nancy does a masterful job raising our consciousness about the importance for women supporting women. The principles outlined in the book help every woman move from success into significance. History teaches us that when women come together and support each other, we can change the world."

—**Trudy Bourgeois,** author of *EQUALITY: Courageous Conversations about Women, Men, and Race to Spark a Diversity and Inclusion Breakthrough*

"We are at a critical point in society where every single woman is needed to engage as a leader. Dr. Nancy O'Reilly takes a hard look at the role that bias plays in advancement, and offers specific strategies to help women uncover personal and workplace bias, realign their perspective, and work together to get ahead. This book is a game changer, and a must-read for women at every level!"

—**Elisa Parker,** cofounder and president of See Jane Do

"*In This Together* is a must-read for women of all races, cultures, and backgrounds. This important and timely book brilliantly details how we as women can inspire and empower one another to build on our strengths and gain success in our workplaces, families, communities, society, and our world."

—**Dr. Sheila A. Robinson,** publisher and CEO of *Diversity Woman* and founder of the Diversity Women's Business Leadership Conference

"This book offers women a powerful perspective about how to advance, how to get support, and how to give support to others."

—**Marlene Chism,** author of *Stop Workplace Drama* and *No-Drama Leadership*

"Dr. O'Reilly's important book shows us how we can grow in our own capabilities and leadership, while at the same time build an empowering culture of mutual respect and support so that we can all work together to reach our highest potential."

—**Kathy Caprino,** MA, founder and president of Ellia Communications and senior *Forbes* contributor

"Nancy O'Reilly's book is inspirational and empowering for all women to read and absorb. These times require women to reclaim their voices and *In This Together* provides the common goals, support, and the pathway to a revolution that is overdue. Feminine leadership is rising and together we can change the world."

—**Danna Beal,** MEd, international speaker and author of *The Extraordinary Workplace: Replacing Fear with Trust and Compassion*

In This
TOGETHER

How Successful Women
Support Each Other
in Work and Life

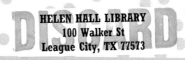

NANCY D. O'REILLY, PsyD
Women Connect4Good, Inc.

Adams Media
New York   London   Toronto   Sydney   New Delhi

Adams Media
An Imprint of Simon & Schuster, Inc.
57 Littlefield Street
Avon, Massachusetts 02322

First Adams Media hardcover edition January 2019

ADAMS MEDIA and colophon are trademarks of Simon & Schuster.

For information about special discounts for bulk purchases, please contact Simon & Schuster Special Sales at 1-866-506-1949 or business@simonandschuster.com.

The Simon & Schuster Speakers Bureau can bring authors to your live event. For more information or to book an event contact the Simon & Schuster Speakers Bureau at 1-866-248-3049 or visit our website at www.simonspeakers.com.

Interior design by Colleen Cunningham

Manufactured in the United States of America

10 9 8 7 6 5 4 3 2 1

Library of Congress Cataloging-in-Publication Data
Names: O'Reilly, Nancy D.
Title: In this together / Nancy D. O'Reilly, PsyD.
Description: Avon, Massachusetts: Adams Media, 2019.
Includes bibliographical references and index.
Identifiers: LCCN 2018038280 | ISBN 9781507208847 (hc) | ISBN 9781507208854 (ebook)
Subjects: LCSH: Leadership in women. | Self-actualization (Psychology) in women. | Helping behavior. | Social movements. | BISAC: BUSINESS & ECONOMICS / Leadership.
Classification: LCC HQ1233 .O74 2019 | DDC 158/.4082--dc23
LC record available at https://lccn.loc.gov/2018038280

ISBN 978-1-5072-0884-7
ISBN 978-1-5072-0885-4 (ebook)

*For all the women who
share their wisdom and experience
to help young women become
the leaders of tomorrow.*

CONTENTS

PART 2
UNWINDING YOUR TWISTED SISTERS
119

CHAPTER 11

ACKNOWLEDGMENTS

" If you want to go fast, go alone. If you want to go far, go together.**"**

UNKNOWN

I thank my agent, Linda Konner, and the entire Adams Media team, including Eileen Mullan, Brendan O'Neill, Laura Daly, Karen Cooper, Frank Rivera, Katie McDonough, Colleen Cunningham, Mary Kate Schulte, and Bethany Carland-Adams. I thank the Women Connect4Good, Inc. team for their diligence, tenacity, vision, persistence, and overwhelming passion. This book would not exist without Maggie Castrey, Cathy Evans, Melissa Miller Young, Cory Goode, and Paul Duckworth. Thanks to Kristal B. Zook and Kate McCracken for their lessons in diversity and inclusion. I'm grateful to the many women who spoke with me privately or in podcast interviews, which are available on my website, DrNancyOReilly .com, including Sarah Acer, Summer Anderson, Laurie Battaglia, Danna Beal, Tabby Biddle, Trudy Bourgeois, Maggie Castro-Stevens, Dr. Claire Damken-Brown, Gloria Feldt, Dr. Lois Frankel, Sharon Hadary, Roxi Hewertson, Judy Hoberman, Regina Huber, Joanna L. Krotz, Cate Montana, Elisa Parker, Linda Rendleman, Terra Renee, Dr. Sheila Robinson, Monique Tallon, and Michele Weldon. I apologize for any inadvertent omissions.

Thanks to my daughters, grandchildren, and great-grandchildren, who may continue this work: Lauren, Leigh, Ragan, Alexis, Isabel, Dain, PJ, Raven, Aspen, Sky, Tristan, and Julian. I thank all of my mentors, those who are still here and those who have passed on, including my grandmothers, Anna and Nancy, and my mother, Phyllis. No one gets anywhere by herself, and I appreciate all the support and help so many have given me. Many blessings to each one of you.

PREFACE

When I started college, I soon fell deeply in love and shortly after found myself married, with a baby, and going to night school. Like many young mothers, I was too busy to spend time with other women and felt painfully lonely. It took me years, and three daughters, to earn my degrees, and I vowed to help my girls avoid feeling as inadequate and isolated as I had. They have consistently connected with other women in support of their values and missions, and have brought seven granddaughters into my life, which I take as a sign that women are my life's work—although I love my grandson and great-grandson just as much.

Women have helped and supported me all along my journey, including eight women students who gave each other moral, physical, and emotional support while we worked on our doctoral degrees and who remain friends to this day. For many years I have worked with a group of wonderful women to provide appropriate work attire for women returning to the workforce, and so far we have helped more than 5,000 women dress to advance at work.

More than a thousand women participated in my research for my first book, *Timeless Women Speak: Feeling Youthful at Any Age*, and I have since heard from thousands more. At my lowest point in life my friends helped me survive. Hundreds of smart, amazing women have spoken with me for podcasts on my website, and nineteen of them coauthored my second book, *Leading Women: 20 Influential*

Women Share Their Secrets to Leadership, Business, and Life. My foundation, Women Connect4Good, Inc., encourages development of women-helping-women networks to raise the status of women and change the world, and we are delighted to partner with Gloria Feldt and Take The Lead, Inc. to achieve gender parity across all sectors by 2025.

All these generous people have shown me that working together with other women is the best way to empower ourselves and have loads of fun in the process. By supporting each other we will step into our power and claim equality for all—together.

—*Dr. Nancy D. O'Reilly, PsyD*

IT'S ABOUT POWER

In January 2017 women stood up together as never before in an action that history will remember simply as "The Women's March." Demonstrating for and against a thousand issues, diverse women gathering around the world drew strength from each other and felt a new thrill of power and solidarity.

In 2018 women continued to escalate their drive to greater power, pay, and influence. It's most obvious in the political realm, where unprecedented numbers of women have run for office and won. Now is the time for women to mentor and support one another at work and in communities around the world. Now is the time to create better lives for everyone.

For those who are still asking, "We marched; now what?" we answer that question resoundingly: it's time for women to support one another in setting their intentions and in carrying out their plans for advancement. Women who have learned to lead in collaborative, caring partnerships create success in business and in life. Together we really can do anything, and in this book we offer tools for earning more, advancing in leadership, and achieving true equality. No one will do this for us. Every human right that women have obtained over the past 250 years—from the right to own property rather than be property, to the rights to hold a job, vote, and run for public office—powerful women warriors have won for themselves. We banded together, strategized, organized, fought, sacrificed, persisted, and at last prevailed. Have all the battles been won? Of course not. Can women work together and join with like-minded people to continue this progress? Of course we can, and we will.

Yet despite today's unprecedented surge of woman power, too many of us still feel anxious and uncertain. We often doubt ourselves, our qualifications, our abilities, our vision, and our right to lead. In this book we explain the ways gender stereotypes undermine women's ability to see themselves as leaders, and then show that the research is crystal clear: companies and organizations that invest in gender equality and promote women to top leadership are more successful, period. According to Vivian Hunt and coauthors in McKinsey & Company's *Delivering Through Diversity* report, when there is gender equality in organizations, teams perform at a higher level and profits are higher. The report states "Companies in the top-quartile for gender diversity on executive teams were 21% more likely to outperform on profitability and 27% more likely to have superior value creation. The highest-performing companies on both profitability and diversity had more women in line (i.e., typically revenue-generating) roles than in staff roles on their executive teams."

The lack of women in so many boardrooms and C-suites, especially the absence of women of color, results not from a shortage of qualifications but from too few opportunities. We are seeing a backlash against women's advances by those who believe that when women gain, they lose. Misogynistic attacks are increasing in politics, communities, and online.

We believe that women working together is the best way to counteract these external forces. This book focuses on overcoming the unconscious or implicit gender biases that limit women's aspirations, intentions, and opportunities.

In Part 1 we remind women of the invaluable strengths they have developed to protect and support their families and build their communities. We discuss why men (both white men and men of color) control the power structures around the world, and we discuss the steps women are taking to overturn the biases that maintain this inequality. We offer specific strategies and language for making that happen. In Part 2 we address another issue exemplified by a question we often receive: "Why is this woman at work so awful to me, and what can I do?" In this part of the book we offer ideas for changing those dynamics, and explain why some women are cruel to each other and what we can do about it. In Part 3 we talk about harassment and violence, "women's issues" that are perpetrated primarily by men. These devastating crimes reinforce the power structure by diminishing and demoralizing the victims, 90 percent of whom are women. We describe strategies that women are using to eliminate such power plays and change the culture. Telling our stories and listening to each other can help us see each other as fully human: women and men of all races, ethnicities, gender expressions, and sexual orientations who can work together.

Women can only reach true equality in the workplace and in society if we identify and partner with others as allies. Historically, any movement to advance women has been done not in spite of men but in partnership with them. Part 3 includes specific strategies and scripts for combatting harassment and violence and engaging willing men to support women's advancement. The Selected Bibliography provides links you can access to learn more.

This book offers combined wisdom from hundreds of individual women and experts whom we found in person, online, and on social media, all eager to share their experiences and advice. We have written it for women of all ages, ethnicities, and sexual orientations, but I think the lessons are useful to everyone who wants to help themselves and others, no matter where they work or live. In the last chapter we issue a call to action for all people of good will to work together to increase women's personal, political, and economic power. What can we unleash when we recognize each woman's diverse path and her perspective of a harmonious world? *Now* is our chance to find out and begin this new adventure—together.

Part 1

USING WOMEN'S STRENGTHS TO ADVANCE

Women have proven their worth for thousands of generations, and these days they're finally demanding—in great numbers—that they receive equal protection and rewards. As actress and singer Janelle Monáe said at the 2018 Grammy Awards, "We come in peace, but we mean business."

I believe women can achieve equal pay, opportunity, advancement, and safety by joining together and asking for what we want. No more believing that women are less than men. No more keeping our heads down and our mouths shut. No more hiding our light and abilities to avoid making others uncomfortable. No more letting others take the credit for our hard work. No more trying not to be noticed to avoid punishment. No more tolerating abuses that destroy the spirits and lives of women and girls. It's time to stop apologizing for being women and start focusing on the strengths we bring to work.

Studies show that companies with more women in top management are more profitable, more successful, and better at recruiting and retaining employees. We'll examine the invaluable strengths that help women succeed as leaders, identify the stereotypes that limit women's advancement, and provide strategies and scripts for handling challenges.

CHAPTER 1
WOMEN WIN WHEN WE SUPPORT EACH OTHER

" Women working together in groups for change is the point. That's what hadn't happened before and that's what's going to make a big difference. **"**

AMY PASCAL, producer and former Sony executive, in *Time*, March 1, 2018

What a thrilling time to work for women's equality! Hundreds of studies have shown that elevating women to power in business, politics, and culture makes life better for *everyone*. The US gender wage gap is below 20 percent for women overall, although that progress doesn't apply equally to women of color. In general, Latina women still have the biggest wage gap compared to white men (nearly 38 percent), then African-American women (32 percent), then white women (18 percent), and Asian women have the smallest gap (7 percent). Even though national progress has slowed in the US, many companies and even entire countries are making pay disparity illegal. Others are insisting that women fill a higher percentage of leadership roles. Sexual harassment is suddenly, officially *not okay* at work. Groups are openly stating their missions to achieve leadership parity for women across all sectors by 2025 or even—gasp—2020!

WHY ARE WE IN THIS TOGETHER?

We have a responsibility and a right to help shape our world into one that offers equal opportunity, pay, and protection to all people, but my special interest is the empowerment of women. The past two hundred years of history have unrolled in an uneven but persistent march toward equality and humanity, driven primarily by women ourselves.

Our Different Experiences Make Us Stronger

It's important for diverse women to work together in this effort because we will all benefit from the power of our full numbers. We draw strength from our diversity, and throughout this book I mean for the words *woman* and *women* to include everyone who identifies as a woman, no matter her gender expression or biological sex. Anger can be a great motivator, and women have plenty of reasons to be angry and frustrated, but we weaken our ability to make change if we allow ourselves to be derailed by our differences. The experiences of women of any ethnicity who occupy a middle or upper socioeconomic class will differ from those of women in the working class. White women have different experiences than women of color. African-American women have different experiences than women of First Nations, Asian, and Latina cultures. Women who do not conform to gender stereotypes have different experiences than cisgender women. Differences like this are real and important, and each woman builds her personality, expresses her identity, sets her goals, and copes with unique barriers within these parameters.

I hope we can acknowledge these differences and at the same time understand how much we all have in common and how much we gain by working together for equality. It's urgent that we support other women because history shows that no one else is going to create this equitable world for us. If we're lucky, men may help us, but we have to lead the way and ask for what we want. One woman alone can't do this, but all of us together, supporting one another, can make it happen. This is where our greatest strength lies.

Focus On Our Successes

Supporting each other is crucial to our success because there are many barriers to the changes we want. The history of the oppression of women, especially women of color, is truly horrifying, and the current state of politics and business is still a long way from our goal. But rather than focus on women's suffering, we choose to focus on our vision of the future because that is where we can create change. And rather than focus on lack, I choose to focus on the abundance I've seen women create when we collaborate and use our power and resources to get things done.

Working together makes us successful because when we come together in groups, we can:

- Clarify our vision and goals
- Learn new ideas, skills, and approaches
- Strategize for success
- Overcome our fears
- Multiply our influence
- Encourage each other and keep our spirits up
- Overcome opposition and punishment
- Provide empathy, compassion, and comfort to those who are grieving
- Improve our health and longevity
- Experience the joy of connection with other human beings

With so many benefits to be had, wouldn't we be crazy not to unite in this common cause of equality for women?

WOMEN'S STRENGTHS, POWER, AND LEADERSHIP

Women possess truly awesome strengths and power that are essential to the human race, not just because women can create babies but because we use our varied abilities to create families, communities, businesses, and nations too. We will talk more about those strengths in Chapter 3. The truth, though, is that despite all our contributions, we have been left out of the power structure. Activist women have long worked to change that, and recent events are evidence that millions of us are ready to help. This is great because hundreds of studies have shown that the more women rise to power in business, politics, and culture, the better life becomes for *everyone* in that community.

Why all this energy and attention now? A resurgence of misogyny, along with the proliferation of cell phones and the megaphone of social media, probably tops the list of influences, but the *real* cause is the brave and determined women who are listening to and supporting each other as never before. Today, millions of women are standing together to demand equal opportunity and safety. Supporting other women has become a really, really good thing.

Women are building on their gains to occupy a greater role in their communities, their nations, and the world because we want to remedy injustices and believe we can make the world better for everyone. Rather than remaining isolated, we are connecting with others, asserting our right to make our own choices and decisions, and committing to changing political and business priorities.

Culture Defines "Feminine" Traits As Low Power

For thousands of years women have been trained by their cultures to behave in certain ways considered to be "feminine." These ideals are expressed differently from culture to culture and can change over time, and everyone has their own definition. Still, our views of ourselves are shaped unconsciously by the dominant culture in which we operate, and studies have shown that the traits considered feminine have a remarkable consistency in cultures around the world.

Gendered norms are powerful human forces, and in general, traits considered to be feminine (for example, submission, affection, sensitivity, and emotion) have not been associated with political or economic status or power. We discuss this at length in the next chapter, but the takeaway here is that women have been excluded from the halls of power because of cultural stereotyping, and because we have developed an unconscious bias against our own abilities. With this book we intend to help women see that their stereotypically "feminine" traits are power tools, not cement shoes.

High-achieving women everywhere have broken that restrictive mold to organize their coworkers, develop successful businesses, and even govern nations, so it's obvious that we can exercise our power. However, these are still exceptions to the rule, and worldwide the vast majority of power positions are still filled by men. In the developed West these are mostly white men; in the rest of the world men of color run the show.

Traditionally, men are expected to be active and aggressive, set the goals, choose the path, execute the vision, and delegate authority. Our culture associates these traits with powerful leaders, so it's natural that men have always been in charge. Right? Wrong! I cringe when I hear women say they don't have any power. We make over 85 percent of purchasing decisions. We have the power of the purse and widespread influence over our families and communities.

Commanding and Inspired Women Leaders

The cultural definition of femininity as powerlessness has stacked the deck against women and made it very difficult for us to ascend into top leadership roles. We can counteract some of this limitation if we focus on the examples of women who are commanding and inspired leaders. Take, for example, Shonda Rhimes. In 2007 *Time* magazine named her one of "100 People Who Shape Our World." As a creator of several hit television series, Rhimes has changed what Americans are watching on television. Her shows place women of color in leading roles and address social issues in every storyline, making for bold programming that changes people's minds. Rhimes is using her personal power to reshape the entertainment industry, which shapes the way we see our world.

Women's work and strengths are needed, used, and valued in business, in the home, in our communities, and across our nations, all of which would collapse without our contributions. Women make up more than half of the total population, have long saturated the ranks of middle management, and have founded some of the most important nongovernmental organizations (NGOs), which I prefer to call social profits instead of not-for-profits. Nearly half of the employees in the US are female, women-owned businesses are the fastest growing segment in our economy, and social profit and philanthropic sectors would grind to a halt without our skills, dogged determination, and labor. We will talk more about the immense value women bring to work in Chapter 3.

About leadership: women lead all the time. We sustain ourselves in the face of adversity, and lead in our families, schools, churches, businesses, neighborhoods, and communities every day. So…if women are so essential to society, and if we lead all the time, everywhere, why have so few of us risen to leadership? Of course, many women have tried to break the glass ceiling; some have succeeded, and entire libraries could be filled with books explaining patriarchal barriers. I'm not minimizing those roadblocks at all; it's clear that they affect diverse women disproportionately, and we need to keep the pressure on by working together for societal change. Our biggest opportunity for change right now, though, is to remove the psychological and emotional barriers *within ourselves* that keep us from seeking the position, power, and authority to make meaningful change.

WHY WOMEN ARE SLOW TO CLAIM OUR POWER

With all our strengths and abilities, and although we have seen a first woman in nearly every role, why do so many women still not see themselves as leaders? Women have fought hard to achieve our current numbers and status:

In the 115th US Congress, elected in November 2016:

- One fifth of members are women (107 women out of 535).
- More than one third of these women (thirty-eight out of 107) are women of color, but they make up only 7 percent of the entire membership.
- Two women members are lesbian or bisexual, which is less than half of 1 percent of all members.

In business:

- One twentieth of *Fortune* 500 CEOs are women (twenty-four in May 2018, including two women of color and zero African Americans, down from an all-time high of thirty-two the previous year).
- 14 percent of executives and top managers at S&P 500 companies are women. We could not find any data about women of color or LGBTQ+ women among S&P 500 companies.

These numbers vary from year to year but have remained consistently low for decades. Modern business and political systems have no financial or other incentives to maintain gender inequality, and world data clearly show that when women participate more in running things, everyone benefits. So why are there still so few women in power positions?

Thought leader and activist Gloria Feldt is the bestselling author of *No Excuses: Nine Ways Women Can Change How We Think About Power*, and cofounder and president of Take The Lead, Inc. She concludes that after generations of subconscious training, women have developed an internal bias against seeing themselves as leaders, and that this is a major factor keeping them from stepping into leadership roles. We discuss this in detail in the next chapter.

Our culture has taught us that leaders, people with power, are men, and even if we consciously reject that idea, our unconscious minds prevent most women from wholeheartedly pursuing those top leadership roles. I spoke once to a group of fifty women attorneys and asked, "Who in this room feels powerful?" These were top-level lawyers, influential in their community, but only two women raised their hands.

In addition to our internal biases against seeing ourselves in business and political leadership roles, women do not feel comfortable in the current leadership structure. The traditional world model of leadership, Feldt teaches, is about having "power over" others. Women have historically been the losers in this oppressive structure, and most women want no part of it. Women have always led *together with others* at every level, so they do not see themselves as leaders in that "power over" model.

"Power Over" Makes a Stressful Workplace

It seems to me that today's business world suffers from an excess of dominating masculine energy and fear-based, conquest-driven leadership. Workplace culture expert Danna Beal called this kind of manager "the boss from hell" and described "him" as ego-driven and elevated to "his" position by keeping his head down, not making waves, saying yes to the right people, and getting promoted because of seniority rather than management skill. We're finally beginning to understand the inherent weakness in this style of leadership.

No one wants to be ordered around in a fear-based workplace, and studies are proving that it's not good business either. Using a single viewpoint to solve problems limits the success of the organization because people are not allowed to participate honestly and openly. Moreover, when they're looking over their shoulders, afraid that they'll make mistakes, the company suffers. Employees lose the initiative to stand out and excel, stifle their own creativity, tend to groupthink, and follow rather than lead. Few will call attention to problems they see for fear of somehow being blamed for or associated with them. This is evidenced by reports that 70 percent of employees in America are disengaged in the workplace, said Beal, citing a Gallup poll, which indicates the need to change organizational cultures.

Women of color in particular are leaving the corporate economy to become entrepreneurs, according to the 2017 American Express *State of Women-Owned Businesses Report*. While the number of women-owned businesses increased by 114 percent from 1997 to 2017, the number of businesses owned by women of color increased by 467 percent. Ownership by individual segments grew even more dramatically than the combined rate: African American (605 percent), Native Hawaiian/Pacific Islander (493 percent), and Latina (491 percent). Business ownership by Asian Americans and Native Americans/Alaskan Natives also grew at higher than average rates

(314 percent and 201 percent, respectively). In addition to disengagement from traditional workplaces, the report states that this trend among women of color is due to their higher unemployment rates, long-term unemployment, sizable pay gap, and the need to *survive*, rather than a desire to seize a market opportunity.

"We attribute the growth in women-owned firms to the lack of fair pay, fair promotion, and family-friendly policies found in corporate America," stated Margot Dorfman, CEO of the US Women's Chamber of Commerce, in an article on Fortune.com. "Women of color, when you look at the statistics, are impacted more significantly by all of the negative factors that women face. It's not surprising that they have chosen to invest in themselves."

"POWER TO" VERSUS "POWER OVER"

Women avoid the "power over" dynamic, but when Feldt redefines power as an expansive collaborative model, as the "power to" do something that is meaningful to them, she says women in her training sessions respond quite differently. In this model, women leaders share responsibility, encourage others to contribute their ideas, ask for advice, make connections among resources and networks, and help each other accomplish goals. In fact, recent studies show that the best chance a woman has of rising higher is to help more women get promoted above her. Supporting women and helping them advance creates more jobs for more women at all levels, which is a good thing because companies with more women are more profitable.

Having just one woman in a company's executive suite reportedly *triples* the number of women promoted to managers. A recent "Getting to Equal" white paper by Accenture, written by Ellyn Shook and Julie Sweet, reported on a survey of 22,000 people in thirty-four countries. Women were promoted at a rate of 23 percent when there was at least one woman in top management, compared to 8 percent when all top roles were filled by men. It also found that women hired with female support at the top were on a fast track and advanced into management within five years.

The success story of Cathy Hughes, founder of Radio One/TV One (now called Urban One), exemplifies this, wrote journalist, author, and professor Kristal Zook in *I See Black People: The Rise and Fall of African American–Owned Television and Radio*. In 1999 Hughes became the first African-American woman to head a publicly traded company. Before she bought her first radio station, in 1980, men in loan departments at thirty-two banks rejected her application. She finally got approval from a Latina who was new to her banking job. When women partner together, we amplify our power.

Using our "power to" enables us to make meaningful change. We can:

- Tap our natural inclination to join together with others
- Gain confidence in our ability to guide and influence the world
- Improve our homes, communities, and businesses
- Help ourselves and others move toward equality in pay, opportunity, and leadership
- Call out bias to create a more equitable world for all
- Focus on the well-being and success of the larger group
- Put forth our best ideas and engage with those around us

When we put all of these positive forces in play, work becomes fun, productive, and much more likely to be successful. Most large businesses today have acknowledged that they urgently need a diverse workforce in order to succeed: hiring employees of all genders, races, and ethnicities to build teams with complementary strengths, better ideas, and problem solving skills. The more women rise to the higher rungs of the ladder, the more profitable the business becomes.

Fortunately, women are learning to use their strengths to gain power and status in a world dominated by men.

Positive Leadership Qualities

Every woman has a wide array of strengths, but what matters most is *how* you do what you do, said Beal. Great leaders focus on "mentoring rather than criticizing, coaching rather than using fear; creating an environment where people know they can make mistakes and be coached into doing better, creating training programs so people really know how to do their jobs, and shadowing other employees," she said. It's often easier for women to take actions like these than it is for men, which may help explain why promoting more women to top leadership makes businesses work better. They create an environment in which people feel empowered to go out and do their very best.

RELATIONSHIPS HELP WOMEN ADVANCE

Women are good relationship builders, a skill they can use to inspire everyone to contribute their best work. Diversity expert Dr. Sheila Robinson, author of *Lead by Example*, is a remarkably inclusive relationship builder, and skilled at networking, mentoring, and sponsoring. I once asked her if people are born to be leaders. She replied that leadership is both natural and learned, often through mentoring.

Mentoring Is Supporting Other Women

Robinson stresses that it's important to give back to your mentors, and one of the best ways is to let them see you follow their advice. But if people worry that they don't have anything to offer their mentor, Robinson tells them, "I asked Dr. Maya Angelou at her kitchen table, 'What can I do for you?' Her response to me was to keep doing what I'm doing. Don't stop." This inspired Robinson to redouble her efforts, and she has since founded a magazine, published a book, and established an annual women's conference, all focused on diversity. She said, "When I talk to my customers and clients to help them understand the value of uniting as we do at the conference, I tell them it's like a cake. If you have all flour or sugar, you've got a mess. You have to have your eggs, your flavoring, sugar, salt, a diverse mix of ingredients to make a wonderful cake."

When women support each other and increase the diversity of their groups, the chemistry is as magical as what turns a diverse mix of ingredients into a cake. So, how do you introduce that collaborative, creative energy into the workplace? It turns out that there's magic in the way women relate together.

WOMEN TEND AND BEFRIEND

The fact that women behave differently than men under stress was confirmed by a woman-led analysis of past research at UCLA. Most psychological research has been conducted by men on other males, and findings have long suggested that men tend to respond to stress with "fight or flight." But the UCLA report, coauthored by Shelley Taylor and published in *Psychological Review*, which examined a wide variety of studies on diverse subjects, confirmed that females' response to stress, in both animals and humans, is much more likely to be "tend and befriend." When there's a crisis at work or at home, women are more likely to show up, clean, fix food, talk, and listen to each other than they are to fight or run away. These are some of the traits that make women the people you want to have around in stressful situations, and I've observed this behavior in others and performed it myself. Life is stressful for women, particularly women of color, and research shows that connecting with others in these ways is good for our health, too, which might be one reason women live longer than men. Is this difference caused by genetics, hormones, evolution, social roles, or conditioning? People can argue this all day, but I believe all of these factors play a role.

Women share skills of problem solving and mutual respect and complement one another's strengths.

All my life I've worked with other women and have observed that you can put five women together in a room, and within an hour they'll have analyzed the problem, made a plan, divided up the action steps, and begun to work toward a solution. Women share skills of problem solving and mutual respect and complement one another's strengths.

Most importantly, though, "tend and befriend" (nurturing others and seeking safety and survival for the group) provides a sustainable model for building successful workplaces and communities. The best thing is that women no longer need to suppress these gifts at work. By using these natural abilities intentionally, we can increase the resiliency of the group and devise effective responses to challenges instead of attacking or ignoring them.

Tend and Befriend in Action

In business tend-and-befriend tactics are the foundation of relationship building, team building, partnering, and sharing the load. In a crisis a strong team supports one another in the face of challenges. Suppose they've worked for months on a project and received approval from management every step of the way, but upon submitting their final proposal they had it torn apart by a manager new to the group. Rather than seeking to place blame or giving up on the project, a team that tends and befriends handles the stressful situation by communicating and encouraging each other, and together devising solutions for a successful outcome.

As a crisis responder, I have observed many people during stressful times, and even in the worst disasters they will stop and help others, sharing when they have little for themselves. Women can calm a hysterical toddler and negotiate a budget to end a government shutdown because they focus on saving other members of the group, not just themselves. That's what's happening when modern women gather to change public policies created primarily by men.

If we all strive every day to work for the well-being and goals of the group, without inserting our individual egos and need for recognition, imagine how that will transform the workplace. It actually takes all of us to create this kind of change. Each of us makes a personal decision about how we will interact with our coworkers, management, and those whom we manage. By aiming for the highest goal and trusting in our strengths, we can respect the opinions of others, learn from different perspectives, and assimilate concern for the greater good into our daily actions.

A challenge for women is that we tend to be more comfortable helping others than asking for help. One day, while recording a podcast interview, I asked my guest how I could support and help her mission. Silence. I finally asked if she was still there. She was astonished and asked, "You mean you want to help me?" I said yes, but even so I had to press her to make a request.

Women often avoid asking for help because they fear being perceived as needy, incompetent, demanding, weak, and not worthy of promotion or respect. We have been taught to conceal our vulnerability. But when we act authentically and invite others to help us solve a problem, we discover strength and power to accomplish things far beyond anything we can do alone.

WOMEN LEADERS SEEK CHANGE

It's hard to find numbers (and honest answers), but people may run for office for a variety of reasons: to avenge a slight, acquire a prestigious job and lifestyle, gain respect, become a well-paid lobbyist after leaving office, impose their will on others, or make a difference in people's lives. However, a survey of members of US state legislatures revealed that the number-one reason women run for office is their concern about one or more specific public policy issues, according to Kira Sanbonmatsu, Susan J. Carroll, and Debbie Walsh in their report *Poised to Run*. Changing public policy on a specific issue is a powerful way to advance a cause. Women who are passionate about a specific cause prove to be highly effective leaders and legislators, and far more than men, they prize results over status, wrote Kelly Dittmar of the Center for American Women and Politics. Identifying a common mission is key to women working together using their "power to."

A good example of this is my own dream team. Every member follows our mission, "Women must support other women," in working together. We foster our relationships, help each other, show appreciation, and take up the slack so each of us can attend to our personal obligations with minimal stress.

The number-one reason women run for office is their concern about one or more specific public policy issues.

I do want to point out that one member of my dream team is a man, so please don't think I'm suggesting that these are exclusively female traits. (Forming alliances with gender-diverse people is crucial, as we discuss in Chapter 9.)

WOMEN'S UNIQUE LEADERSHIP ROLE

Trying to imitate a man's leadership style doesn't make sense to leadership coach and author Roxi Hewertson. In our podcast interview she told me that her first rule is "It's ALL about relationships." Women need to use their many skills in a "leaderly mindful way" that is both process- and results-oriented. Results matter, of course, while attention to the process can ensure that people feel respected, heard, and valued. She said women are "born with a brain that understands emotional intelligence. We just need to remember that we aren't in competition with men or each other. We do best when we own our strengths."

Today's organizations need diverse points of view and problem-solving styles to succeed. It's up to those in power to give diversity more than lip service and recognize our wide variety of human strengths as a resource for leadership. Cate Montana told me in our podcast interview that she had adopted a completely masculine style while working in network sports and journalism because she was competing in an arena where few women worked. She was changed by an eye-opening interview with a shaman from the Shuar tribe in the Amazon rainforest. He described his tribe's system, in which men and women work consciously with one another's strengths rather than playing upon each other's weaknesses. His people completely understood the characteristics of masculine and feminine natures. "In my tribe, men and women have equal say, equal authority on tribal council, are equally respected. We do have a highly segmented society. Men do men things—they hunt and fish and cut down trees, etc.—and women take care of the domestic side of life. But there is one job that the women do, and the tribe's survival depends on it." Montana responded automatically, "Yeah, okay, babies." And he said, "No, that's not it. This goes far beyond our biology. Men understand that the masculine, by its nature, tends to be more aggressive, linear, focused, task-goal-oriented and very competitive. And we know, as men, that we will hunt until there is nothing left to kill. We will fish until there's nothing left in the rivers. We will cut down trees until there's nothing left standing. We also understand that woman is more intuitive, more grounded in nature, connected with community and its needs, and that includes the needs of nature. So, the men desperately lean on and depend on the women to tell them when to stop."

Montana realized then that she had been so conditioned to act like a guy, work like a guy, and set goals like a guy that she had no more idea of how to stop than any man. The shaman observed that our so-called "developed nations" are so busy doing and striving and competing and depleting resources that this driving masculine nature is taking the whole world over a cliff. Then he asked her, "Where are your women? Why are they not telling their men to stop?"

Balanced Leadership Creates Success

Effective leadership in our workplaces, as in the Shuar tribe, relies on a balance of women's and men's leadership styles—sometimes expressed as yin (yielding/soft) and yang (forceful/hard). Women need to trust their strengths and use them to create successful working environments. Many men are wonderful leaders and very supportive of women's equality at their companies, and all of us can engage yin and yang, feminine and masculine, energies to lead effectively.

When her boss left, Monique Tallon applied for and got her boss's job leading large conferences for eBay. As she told me in our podcast interview, she was in her early twenties, had no experience, and didn't have a clue what to do. She took a risk, revealed her vulnerability (a yin skill), and asked her team to help. It worked because she was able to create a connection with them and immediately built trust, and they helped her pull off a huge event.

Women need to trust their strengths and use them to create successful working environments.

Tallon said that it was a turning point for her. "I realized that when women tap into their strengths, like empathy, vulnerability, stepping into other people's shoes, really empowering others, listening to them, and caring about them, people respond well." Global surveys have shown that people want their leaders to demonstrate compassion, caring, vision, passion, empathy, and vulnerability. Since women have an abundance of those abilities, Tallon advised women to leverage those qualities.

When Women See Themselves As Leaders

Women need to imagine themselves as leaders before they can aspire to leadership roles at work and in communities. The drawback is that often women don't see what they do as leadership even though many are leaders every day. Dr. Sheila Robinson said, "A mother is a leader with her children. She influences how her children go out into the school. Anytime you have the power to influence something that is going to impact your community, society, and the world, you are a leader."

Women have unlimited inner power, but they are unaware of it, said transformational leadership coach and author Regina Huber when I interviewed her. "We have to connect with that inner power to accomplish our goals." However, women are stuck in thinking we're not enough, that what we have to say isn't important. Huber is on a quest to help women change that. Women must see the value of what we bring to the table as authentic human beings and exercise "courage to bring the feminine element to the world of business." In our businesses, communities, and families, Huber said, "women have been brought up to blend in. As long as we blend in, others will get the promotions. Leaders don't blend in. They stand out." In charting our paths as leaders, women can gather courage from each other.

FIND YOUR SUPPORT GROUP

Women have always come together in supportive communities, like quilting bees, prayer groups, book clubs, bond drives, lunch bunches, political campaigns, and fund-raisers. We draw on the support of people united by a shared interest. As you navigate the often-confusing world of work, it helps to find or build a supportive community of women. Whether this group is small or large, formal or casual, work related or community based, local or international, it's where you can find reassurance, confidence, hope, ideas, and joyful connections.

When I say that women are "in this together," I hope you will feel inspired to:

- Support other women
- Perceive your womanly instincts/inclinations as strengths
- Help each other develop self-confidence to use those strengths
- Claim your "power to" take your place as a leader in an expansive, collaborative model
- Work together with others to make a better world

In this book we will explore the whys and hows of using our numbers, our abundant women's strengths, and our "power to" overcome the barriers. We have so much to gain by working together, and this book will explain where we have come from, where I hope we are going, and how we can get there. I honestly believe that we can create the equitable world we want and need, together.

CHAPTER 2
HOW BIAS WORKS AGAINST EQUALITY

❝ The emotional, sexual, and psychological stereotyping of females begins when the doctor says: It's a girl.**❞**

SHIRLEY CHISHOLM, second African-American woman in the New York State legislature and the first to run for a major party's presidential nomination

Over thousands of years humans have developed ideas about what people are like, and who is good at what, and we use these to keep order in our world. Gender stereotypes don't just describe how men and women *do* behave; they prescribe how we *should* behave within the dominant culture. Society says that if we don't follow the rules, we will be punished. For example, if a couple decides that Mom will work her way into the C-suite while Dad stays home with the children (counter to "normal" roles), they face suspicion and criticism for breaking out of traditional gender behavior. These ideas live in a deep unconscious place in our brains.

In the not-too-distant past many young women entering college were also encouraged to go after a "Mrs. Degree" by catching a high-earning man who would make a good provider. The notion of creating their own well-paying careers was too ridiculous to consider. A friend of mine had a college professor in 1968 who derided her anxieties about her senior thesis by saying, "Why do you care? You're just going to get married anyway." The package of money, security, and reproduction with a well-heeled man was still regarded as ideal back then.

By now much has changed, and the pace of change is accelerating. Women of all gender identities are choosing diverse relationship types, including remaining single and not having children. They are no longer willing to accept their lack of progress into executive roles, their lagging salaries, and ongoing barriers at work. Still, the persistence of stereotypes and sexism means that women walk a tightrope.

FACT: WE ALL HAVE BIASES

It's hard to see and talk about the stereotypes that create gender bias because we have absorbed them with every breath since birth. Some of these are internal and limit the aspirations and expectations we have for ourselves as women. Leadership development expert and author Trudy Bourgeois told me, "You don't know what you don't know." She said that if we are to create equality for all women, we have to name our biases and talk about them. Biases are the automatic beliefs and thoughts that drive our actions, deriving from things we've been socialized to believe, say, and do. The brain creates biases as shortcuts to help categorize and make sense of our world. Today, women who want to rise at work are challenging traditional gender roles, which makes some people very uncomfortable. As we work through these challenging feelings, we need to remember to ask for what we want, work together with other women, and believe in our ability to create a more equitable world.

Our culture has for a long time assigned men to every power position, so it's no surprise that we automatically attribute authority to males and see women's helping roles as normal. I don't believe that men plotted together to establish a patriarchy, although I do think that plenty of men today are strongly motivated to maintain it.

Men certainly still run the worlds of business and politics, but many women are in denial about this because they just can't believe that gender bias is still so widespread. This denial undermines their ability to work for equality. Numerous studies have proven that gender bias exists—for example, when more men are hired to play in symphonies than women, but the difference disappears when musicians audition behind a screen; or when men are judged as job applicants to be more competent than women who have been trained to perform exactly the same script and behavior. You doubtless have your own list of gender biases that you have witnessed or experienced in your own career.

> If we are to create equality for all women, we have to name our biases and talk about them.

All women today are accountable for learning to overcome their internal biases so they can expand their aspirations and support rather than stand in the way of other women. Despite our best efforts, as we have watched other women fight against bias in order to better themselves, many women have been reluctant to support their efforts honestly and with an open heart. We automatically make unconscious judgments about each other within seconds and are slow to change those opinions. We humans are funny that way.

I will warn you that people may not thank you for pointing out the stereotypes and biases at play in their relationships, so prepare yourself to deal with some defensiveness and denial, even from the most open-minded people you know. Most of us do not want to believe that we are prejudiced about anything or anybody. We can help others understand these issues by sharing how awareness of our own biases has surprised and then helped us.

WHERE GENDER STEREOTYPES COME FROM

Our fixed ideas about gender usually operate below our level of awareness, as unconscious or implicit biases that shape our attitudes and behaviors. We all have these lurking in our minds, and they limit our roles, relationships, aspirations, and progress at work. It's easy for us to see attitudes in other people that hold women back, but it's much harder for us to perceive the ways we limit ourselves.

Stereotypes, the handy short-cuts that our brains create to help us make quick decisions in daily living, cause problems when we don't notice how they distort our worldview and prevent us from forming healthy relationships with others. The initial social function of gender stereotypes may have been to ensure that *someone* raises the children and *someone* provides for them. When these stereotyped gender roles spill into our work lives, though, they limit women's ability to advance.

> **❝** Implicit bias refers to the attitudes or stereotypes that affect our understanding, actions, and decisions in an unconscious manner. **❞**
>
> KIRWAN INSTITUTE,
> The Ohio State University

The Genders Really Aren't All That Different

Some people believe that our genetics determine gender differences. They see people of different genders as fundamentally different in attitudes, abilities, and behavior. Researchers have shown, however, that genetics account for only a few consistent differences between genders. When it comes to our behaviors, thousands of studies reveal far more similarities than differences across genders. All people possess both masculine and feminine qualities. Guess what. They are all *human* qualities.

For example, cisgender men (who identify with the gender assigned to them at birth) are typically bigger and stronger, more interested in casual sex, and more physically violent than women. That's about it. Researcher Janet Shibley Hyde, known for her research on human sexuality, sex differences, gender, and development, analyzed thousands of studies. Her results, published in *American Psychologist*, showed that behaviors across genders overlap with 85 percent similarity and only 15 percent difference. This means that most of those judgments—that men are good at this and women excel at that, including the assumptions made by you, your boss, and generations of researchers—are based on unfounded stereotypes.

Learning to Perform Gender

But don't people of different genders behave very differently? Absolutely. But those behaviors are not inherent in our genetic makeup; they are learned. Society enforces these gendered traits with rewards and punishments, a program that begins in infancy. Children are programmed to seek their parents' approval in order to survive, and they quickly become skilled at performing their gendered roles based on how their parents respond. For example, a boy who's scolded for wanting nail polish might not ask for it again; a girl who hates dresses might comply by wearing them if her parents tell her she should. I once watched a young woman call her two-year-old son "little man" and refer to her daughter as a "princess." Which one do you think will grow up to be brave and have a voice?

When boys receive approval from birth for their aggression and adventurousness, they feel entitled to lead and dominate. When girls receive approval for their warmth and cooperation, they feel most comfortable in nurturing roles, which incidentally carry a lower status and lower pay.

Even very young children will reject clothing, playthings, and games that "belong" to another gender. This conformity strengthens the myths of gendered differences, and society's pressures to live up to these norms actually increase as we move through puberty and into adulthood. In a culture in which men occupy all the power positions, most girls quickly learn to accommodate the men in power in order to survive.

Gender Stereotypes for Women

Everyone wants to be loved, and different cultures establish their own criteria for what makes women lovable. Many women enjoy performing traditionally "feminine" behaviors focused around hair, makeup, and fashion, and our culture teaches us that the most important thing about women is our appearance. To be considered "feminine," women in most cultures have also been expected to behave in stereotypical ways (for example, submissive, superstitious, affectionate, dreamy, sensitive, attractive, dependent, emotional, fearful, weak, sexy, gentle, sentimental—you get the idea). A study by John E. Williams and Deborah L. Best showed that these traits were considered feminine in twenty out of twenty-five countries around the world, including North and South America, Europe, Africa, and Asia.

Our point is not that women are or are not any of these things, but that the feminine "brand" has been draped with such characteristics, all of which have been associated with likability in addition to low power and status. To be sure, millions of women draw deep satisfaction, worth, and status from playing out traditional women's roles and attitudes. But women who are single parents, heads of their own households, working to provide for their families, or seeking to feel respected and valued in positions outside the home must fill different roles.

Subcultures create variations on these themes. Many African-American communities, for example, have a more matriarchal system than white American cultures, due to a history of families destroyed through slavery, continued racism and poverty, and generations of mass incarceration of black men. African-American women bear the burden of continued racism and oppression that whites do not experience, and many fear for the survival of their men and boys. Women of color may revel in their femininity while providing the fierce and powerful glue that holds family, church, and community together, and within their subculture they can be accorded high honor and respect. Outside their communities, however, they receive less power and opportunity than white women.

Again, our point here is not that women are or are not stereotypically "feminine," but that women's roles are not accorded status, respect, or power in the dominant culture. Most women have internalized this on some level, and it affects our self-esteem even if we consciously reject those judgments. Many have hidden who they are or hardened themselves to survive. When I think of what "feminine" means, I think of women's skill in building relationships and connecting and collaborating with others. To me, our ability to see into the heart of issues and solve problems is feminine. It's good to get clear on our own definition and to understand how our ideas differ from those of the dominant culture.

Gender Stereotypes for Men

Williams and Best studied traits considered masculine around the world too. Here are some of the traits considered masculine in twenty out of twenty-five countries: adventurous, dominant, forceful, independent, strong, aggressive, autocratic, daring, enterprising, courageous, and active. All these traits are associated with being respected and accorded power rather than being liked. As researcher Janet Shibley Hyde discovered, though, men and women are 85 percent similar in their behaviors and only 15 percent different. We all have "masculine" and "feminine" traits, so it's clear that the lists reflect cultural stereotypes, not reality.

These gender stereotypes severely restrict men's lives by trapping them in a toxic masculinity that cuts them off from normal expression of emotion, nurturing behaviors, and the development of meaningful relationships. In recent decades energy has been gradually building behind a men's movement to dismantle this toxic masculinity and allow them to express the full range of their humanity too. Men stand to gain as much as women from greater equality, as we will discuss in Chapter 9.

Relationships Create Confusion

The fact that people love and need each other makes sorting out stereotypes extra complicated and confusing for everyone. As sociologists Peter Glick and Susan Fiske pointed out in their article "Ambivalent Sexism," men dominate women, but they also depend on them for all kinds of support and fulfillment, just as women depend on men. This interdependence creates ambivalence and conflict all around.

Traditional attitudes are changing—for example, most people would agree that it's fine for women today to play sports and want big, well-paying jobs—but deep-seated bias lurks under the surface and shapes the ways people perceive and treat each other. People still act on gender stereotypes in many sexist ways to define and limit others. Our special interest here is the many ways that sexist attitudes limit women.

TYPES OF SEXISM

Sexism is a term that describes attitudes that disadvantage women and are often held by women as well as men. Three main types affect women: benevolent, hostile, and internalized. All three affect women at work and in life. In Chapter 4 we will examine some ways that women can respond to these attitudes.

Benevolent Sexism

Benevolent sexism features attitudes that seem like friendly concern but that actually reward women for being nice and compliant and not resisting domination by men. I want to spend the most time on this one because it's insidious and the hardest for women to resist. "Kind of seems like a compliment, even though it's rooted in men's feelings of superiority," Alia E. Dastagir noted in her 2018 *USA Today* article "A Feminist Glossary Because We Didn't All Major in Gender Studies." "It's when men say women are worthy of their protection (off the sinking boat first) or that they're more nurturing than men (therefore should raise children). It's restrictive."

> **"We have a word for power over women: sexism."**
>
> GLORIA FELDT,
> activist

For example, directing women into public relations because they are great communicators puts them at a corporate dead end. Women who are gracious and welcoming get saddled with organizing all the office events. Women who are intuitive and connect well with others are expected to manage the office's emotional housework, including relational aggression among other women. Finally, men who refuse to travel for business with women prevent them from advancing higher in sales or management. Taking that even further, the so-called "Mike Pence rule" prevents a man from being alone with any woman other than his wife, to avoid the temptation for romantic or sexual involvement and/or to prevent accusations of impropriety or harassment. This defines women as either romantically irresistible or as lying accusers. Either interpretation severely limits women's opportunities for advancement.

Women can actually benefit from benevolent sexism but in a short-term and complicated way. "A woman who insists that a date open doors for her and pay for dinner or feigns hysteria to get a man to catch a mouse may get what she wants in the immediate situation," wrote sociologists Laurie A. Rudman and Peter Glick in their fascinating text *The Social Psychology of Gender*. "Unfortunately, however, she has also reinforced gender stereotypes and paternalistic condescension."

Hostile Sexism

Hostile sexism overtly punishes women for straying from narrow, traditional roles and threatening men's primacy. Open insults, objectification, degradation, and physical and sexual assault have been the fate of women pioneers in various men-dominated workplaces, including manufacturing, law enforcement, firefighting, and the military. This is the easiest form of sexism to identify, although until recently it was still very difficult to fight.

As a psychological intern at a Federal Medical Center that serves US prisons, I encountered male correctional officers who made it clear that I did not belong there. They made it difficult for me to do my job. I was literally locked down in dangerous places within the prison. I had to learn to fit in, to hang out and talk with the correctional officers so that we were buddies. They stopped locking me up and I survived my internship, safe but very angry.

Internalized Sexism

Internalized sexism occurs when the belief in women's inferiority becomes part of a woman's own worldview and self-concept. This can severely limit a woman's aspirations and cause her to condemn and obstruct other women who want to break out of gendered roles.

In a personal email in May 2018 social psychologist Peter Glick wrote to my team, "I think that White women's support for Trump in the election (they were way more likely to support Trump on average than minority women were) shows how some women still have a strong stake in the current gender hierarchy. Men are still seen as the protectors and providers by a good number and this benevolent sexism is more subtle, socially supported, and difficult to combat."

Women's stake in the gender hierarchy might consist of maintaining their comfort level, avoiding the unknown, obeying religious requirements, or a fear of disrupting the system in which they have gained and learned to wield power. Suzanne Moore wrote in *The Guardian* that she would wager that every woman who dismissed Trump's treatment of women as just "the way men are" has also defended a man in her life who has done the same thing. Whether seeking protection, adoration, or to stay true to their religious values, these women are comfortable in their "rightful" position. Anything that deviates from their norms is considered unnatural and against divine law.

Women can encounter benevolent, hostile, and internalized sexism simultaneously in the same work setting and even in the same individual. In Chapter 4 we examine some ways women can overcome these forces.

The Goldilocks Syndrome

No matter what women do, someone will judge their performance as either too hot or too cold but almost never just right. Consider the legal cases of Ann Hopkins in 1989 and Shelley Weinstock in 2000. Together they demonstrated that career women can be penalized either way, whether they act in stereotypically feminine ways or not.

Ann Hopkins, a highly successful accountant at Price Waterhouse, had brought the firm more business than any other candidate and was the only woman in a pool of eighty-eight accountants seeking to become partners. Despite her stellar performance, Hopkins was denied the partnership that she had clearly earned because, she said, the other partners told her she was too abrasive and needed a course in charm school. According to her lawsuit, Price Waterhouse v. Hopkins, 490 U.S. 228, 87-1167 (Supreme Court of the United States 31 October 1988), the other partners advised her to learn to "walk more femininely, talk more femininely, dress more femininely, wear makeup, have her hair styled, and wear jewelry." A single mother of three, she quit the company, then sued all the way to the Supreme Court and won.

In contrast, chemistry professor Shelley Weinstock was denied tenure by Columbia University even though the administrators at Barnard College, where she worked, recommended that tenure be granted. She claimed that she heard herself described as an outstanding example of a nice and nurturing woman and maintained that Columbia's administrators could not credit her with also being a good researcher and scholar, even though her record made clear that she was all those things. Her application for tenure was denied, as were her subsequent suit and appeals in federal courts, according to a review of the case on AAUW.org. As Rudman and Glick, authors of *The Social Psychology of Gender*, explained, evaluators reinforce their implicit biases against women's advancement by "switching their focus to a woman's niceness when it undermines her competence and to her assertiveness when it undermines her interpersonal skills."

Stereotypes can enforce racial discrimination as well. African-American women continue to sue today for the right to wear their hair naturally (in braids or Afros) rather than being forced to process it so that it is straight and conforms to white cultural norms. In 2014 their pressure caused the US military to expand its grooming guidelines to permit women to wear their hair in twists and to remove the words "matted and unkempt" from regulations.

Evaluations for hiring are just as complex as those for advancement, as national studies show. For example, when a man's name was attached to a résumé, evaluators scored the applicant higher on competence and hire-ability and offered a higher salary and more professional mentorship than when a woman's name was attached to the identical résumé. It's not even a man thing, reported Erika Christakis in *Time*. Women evaluators were just as strongly biased in favor of candidates they perceived as men, an example of internalized sexism.

While I worked to complete my education, I was more than once criticized for my competitiveness. I had dreams, I had goals, but those things made me appear unwomanly and not nice. I doubt I would have been criticized for this if I had been a man.

Burden of the Second Shift

A major factor holding back women at work is the burden of the "second shift" at home. Heterosexual married women have been acculturated not to expect their husbands to help, and women will do up to three-fourths of home chores before they balk, wrote Rudman and Glick. Even when husbands are willing to pitch in, their wives may undermine this role shift. They doubt their spouse will do it properly, demean their spouse's abilities, and continue to insist on doing it themselves. In her book *Drop the Ball*, Tiffany Dufu, chief leadership officer at Levo, calls this "home control disease." It's hard for many women to release their stranglehold on traditional roles when their self-image is closely tied to these gender roles. The luxury of hiring help isn't an option for women who can't afford it, so persuading a partner to help is their only hope for reducing the burden of the second shift. Of course, single parents must shoulder the full load alone.

The second shift includes not just tasks but also emotional labor. Women immediately understand the unequal weight of running a home, family, or workplace, but men rarely understand it. "All you have to do is ask me to help," a good man will say, but his partner doesn't want to have to ask. If she still has to think it through and delegate assignments, it means that those jobs are her responsibility, not his. It's as if he is doing her a favor rather than doing his share. "I don't want to micromanage housework. I want a partner with equal initiative," wrote Gemma Hartley in *Harper's Bazaar*. "We find all kinds of ways in society to ensure that girls and women are responsible for emotions and, then, men get a pass." Hartley, who works a full-time job, once asked her husband to arrange for a housecleaning service as a Mother's Day present so that "for once I would not be in charge of the household office work. I would not have to make the calls, get multiple quotes, research and vet each service, arrange payment and schedule the appointment....The clean house would simply be a bonus." (He didn't, and the story itself is worth a read, but she isn't giving up.)

It's hard for many women to release their stranglehold on traditional roles when their self-image is closely tied to these gender roles.

Hartley admitted that she's better at this emotional labor and enjoys it more than her husband because she has skills developed over a lifetime. Women often have a pleasant history of sharing kitchen time with Mom or Grandma, and many derive genuine satisfaction from tending to their loved ones. However, she pointed out, her husband has "a whole lot of life left to hone his emotional labor skills, and to change the course of our children's future. Our sons can still learn to carry their own weight. Our daughter can learn to not carry others." By shedding our preconceived ideas about gender and demonstrating equality at home, we can move women a giant step forward in a single generation.

Most women today no longer consciously believe that their primary job is to be a loving nurturer of the men who go forth to accumulate all the power, leaving women on the bottom. "This is not to suggest that loving and nurturing are wrong, but only to ask why women are expected to do the lion's share of it," stated Rudman and Glick. Some regard this as a radical thought because "the alternative—viewing women as persons in their own right—would require that men equally shoulder the burden of caring for others and afford women an equal voice in governing their private and public worlds." Does this sound reasonable to you or impossible?

WHEN WOMEN HAD POWER

It hasn't always been like this, as Hannah Devlin wrote in *The Guardian*. She reported on a scientific study that found humans used to live in egalitarian hunter-gatherer groups, societies that had gendered divisions of labor but few restrictive gender roles. Devlin explained that gender "equality may have proved an evolutionary advantage for early human societies, as it would have fostered wider-ranging social networks and closer cooperation between unrelated individuals." Indeed, these are advantages we still see today in companies where woman help lead. Women held equal status, helped each other get the job done, and were appreciated for their many strengths and abilities, which complemented those of all genders. These cultures have been described as "Goddess" cultures because, unlike today, women had considerable power. Patriarchy rose around 6,000 years ago, reported writer and director Tiffany Shlain in her wonderful short film *50/50: Rethinking the Past, Present & Future of Women + Power*. As patriarchy rose, women's status fell. Women's role became primarily caring for home and children, bringing rewards for collaborative traits like nurturing, friendliness, and expressiveness. Men, in contrast, worked outside the home to acquire resources and power, and build alliances with other men. Patriarchy is still our current system, in which men occupy nearly all the power positions. It's been around long enough that many people see it as divinely ordained and cannot imagine any other system.

Reclaiming Women's Stories

One consequence of men holding all the power positions was the silencing of the voices of women, their near-elimination from written history. A horrifying example of this silencing was hundreds of years of witch trials that took place in Europe and the US beginning in the seventeenth century. Shlain also stated in her film that an estimated fifty thousand women in Europe and the American colonies were burned or drowned for various offenses, which I suspect included stepping outside of gender norms. I could easily believe, as some have said, that many were women of color working as midwives, herbalists, and spiritual healers whose power was regarded as extremely threatening.

Women of color have also been crucial to every women's and human rights movement in the US and almost never get credit for their extraordinary contributions.

Women working together are telling these lost stories. I was delighted to see the success of *Hidden Figures*, the film about women physicists and computer experts of color who were essential to the success of Apollo 11 and the US space program. Not only had history entirely omitted the contributions Margaret Hamilton, Katherine Johnson, and others made to NASA projects in the 1950s and 1960s, but it's also clear that those women's roles were minimized and kept hidden even when their work was essential to the success of the collective mission. Women of color have also been crucial to every women's and human rights movement in the US and almost never get credit for their extraordinary contributions. Artist and illustrator Ellen Schaeffer wanted her adolescent daughter to learn more about inspiring women, so she painted portraits, wrote bios, and developed 118 trading cards about women of all colors who were trailblazers in social justice, STEM careers, literature, and the arts. She calls them Persistent Sisters and distributes them nationwide.

Whose experience is missing from the stories you tell? Could you tell more diverse stories in a newsletter, in social media posts, or through the speakers you invite to groups? Could you attend social events sponsored by other groups, or invite diverse women to yours? What other ways might you increase the opportunities for them to be heard?

Social Pressures Change Gender Roles

For the past two hundred years major social changes have rapidly transformed women's roles in the world, leaving people of all genders feeling dazed and confused by new rules and expectations. Two centuries ago American women had the legal and political status of children, explained Harvard University sociologist Robert Max Jackson in his book *Destined for Equality*. Women and children were chattel, the property of men. Boys grew up to be persons, but girls did not. Only single women were allowed jobs outside the home, and higher education and the professions were closed to women. Divorce was allowed only rarely, women were not allowed to control their own reproduction, and their sphere was virtuous control over the home.

The first women's rights convention happened in Seneca Falls, New York, in 1848. As the century unfolded, women began to successfully sue for divorce and gained near-equal roles in rugged western states, including voting rights. Seventy-one years after that first convention American women won the national right to vote with the passage of the nineteenth amendment, but it was well into the 1960s before many women of color were able to exercise that right. Through the twentieth century women have continued to organize and work together, and we've won the right to apply for any job, attend any school, have credit in our own names, run for office, and run a business.

Women who did these things provided models that other women wanted to emulate. Rosie the Riveter showed that women could manufacture planes and fly them, and education opened doors that could not be closed. The arrival of oral contraceptives in the 1960s was arguably the biggest game changer for women, because for the first time they could choose when—and if—they would bear a child. As women's expectations and aspirations have broadened, we have begun to see that we have options, and I have noticed that power accrues to those who have choices. Empowerment means helping women get access to, perceive, and exercise choice. Each of these societal changes created conflicts with traditional gender stereotypes. Today, women are pursuing parity in political office, equity in men-dominated workplaces, equal access to high-status professions, equal treatment after divorce, and punishment of sexual harassment and rape. This is astounding progress, for which we are profoundly grateful.

> Power accrues to those who have choices. Empowerment means helping women get access to, perceive, and exercise choice.

Make no mistake, none of the gains of the past two centuries were *given* to women by men. Far from it. Women have worked and strategized and organized and persuaded and sacrificed—together—to make these changes.

Punishing Gender Violations

It's always risky to be a woman pioneer (hello, double standard). "The strongest backlash effects seem to be directed at powerful women," noted Rudman and Glick. "An Internet search for images of powerful women…reveals many that caricature them as monsters or demean them through what has been colorfully dubbed 'political pornography,' sexualized images in which a powerful woman is shown getting her 'comeuppance.'" These punishments typically cast doubt on a woman's femininity and her ability to attract a man, which are central to a woman's traditional role.

MAKING PRIVILEGE VISIBLE

In order for women to work together to achieve success, we must acknowledge our own unconscious biases. Many of us are hyperconscious of the privilege that entitles men to jobs, respect, and sex, and creates an inability to see gender discrimination. But straight, white, cisgender women, and anyone who is part of a dominant majority culture, may be equally unable to see the privilege they possess.

> In order for women to work together to achieve success, we must acknowledge our own unconscious biases.

In a TED Talk sociology professor Michael Kimmel recalled a woman of color in a seminar asking a white woman, "When you wake up in the morning and you look in the mirror, what do you see?" "I see a woman," said the white woman. The other woman replied, "When I wake up in the morning and I look in the mirror, I see a black woman. To me, [my] race is visible," she said. "But to you, [your] race is invisible. You don't see it. That's how privilege works. Privilege is invisible to those who have it." The privilege of not seeing your own race or sexuality, or not having to question your gender, comes from belonging to a group deemed "normal" or "typical" in the dominant culture. In the US straight, white people who identify with the gender they were assigned at birth are "normal" and everyone else is considered "abnormal."

Dangers of Groupthink

When people get frustrated, a common human response is to direct their anger at someone else. Psychologists see this with people in therapy, and it is the opposite of taking responsibility for oneself. Our human need to feel included causes us to embrace a group mind. This collective action phenomenon causes people to adopt the views, opinions, and behaviors of the group, even when they contradict our personal beliefs. Man-woman mistrust has a lot in common with racial and religious prejudice, and with suspicion and resentment among socioeconomic classes. All are based on unconscious biases instilled in us by society.

This tendency to want to separate ourselves from and blame the "other" may explain why groups so rarely work together against forces holding them down. People in power may work consciously to divert our anger and attention from them and keep us fighting among ourselves. Our internalized biases make many of our associates enablers too. It's not just that it's "easier" to blame a peer; it's really hard to organize and collaborate on a major societal change. People have to stand firm in the face of opposition and condemnation, including threats from people they love, admire, and depend on. It's scary and dangerous to fight the status quo, as the civil rights movement in the US demonstrated. The scapegoat changes with the moment (immigrants, any faith different from one's own, people of color, people living in poverty, people with mental illness or drug addiction, fat people, homeless people, homosexuals, feminists, any tribe different from one's own, many other groups), but all have been blamed at one time or another for causing society's ills. Our unconscious biases keep us focusing on our differences and placing blame.

Intersectionality = Layers of Discrimination

As we work to gain equality, let's build bridges and make common cause with others who are different from ourselves. This requires us to understand each other. Clearly, an elderly transgender black woman faces a different set of prejudices at work than a young cisgender white woman. *Intersectionality*, a term developed by legal scholar Kimberlé Crenshaw, describes the way different systems of power disproportionally affect people who identify as members of more than one marginalized community. None of us is just one thing, but too often inclusion in one group erases our ability to fight discrimination based on other aspects of our identity.

For example, Crenshaw wrote in an article for *The Washington Post* that such erasure is experienced by "people of color within LGBTQ movements; girls of color in the fight against the school-to-prison pipeline; women within immigration movements; trans women within feminist movements; and people with disabilities fighting police abuse—all face vulnerabilities that reflect the intersections of racism, sexism, class oppression, transphobia, ableism and more."

Seeing and Understanding Differences

In learning about people whose experiences are different from our own, Crenshaw said we must recognize that women are not, in fact, all the same, nor do they all feel a certain way. Become conscious of language that leaves out others and choose words with inclusion in mind. Ask if the differences in your workplace are represented in management and leadership, and take the time to form relationships with people whose identities and experiences are different from yours. The responsibility to educate yourself is your own and begins with developing an authentic relationship with a person you want to get to know. "If you are unsure about a concept or want to learn more about a specific intersection of identity, Google it!" Crenshaw wrote in *YW Boston Blog*. Remember to read critically, though, since the quality of information on the Internet varies dramatically. If you have a question about something you read, consider respectfully asking the person you are getting to know to tell you their perspective. As Trudy Bourgeois wrote in her book *Equality*, people love to talk and share their stories, so the first step is to become more inquisitive and curious about the lives of others. Stereotypes are obviously inaccurate and ridiculous when they apply to us, so how hard is it to believe that they are inaccurate and ridiculous when they apply to others? Don't assume that you know what someone else's life is like. Ask what their life is like and open up to new understanding.

Color Bias

In 1967, when NBC's Sander Vanocur asked the Reverend Martin Luther King Jr. what differentiates African Americans from other ethnic groups of immigrants, the term *intersectionality* hadn't yet been coined. Even so, King's answer made clear the burden of the layers of discrimination imposed on African Americans. "White America must see that no other ethnic group has been a slave on American soil," he said. No other immigrant group was brought here in chains and made to work for 244 years for free. When they were freed, they received no help to establish independent lives, no land, no shoes, even in a time when the US government was giving away millions of acres of land to white European immigrants. Plus, their color was deliberately stigmatized. Into the present day formerly enslaved peoples continue to be limited by a denial of civil rights, police violence, frequent incarceration, and other punishments for simply engaging in community life. These significant disadvantages are still inflicted upon people of color today and greatly restrict opportunities.

King did not mention gender bias, but Shirley Chisholm once said that she found her gender to be a particular setback in politics. "I met more discrimination as a woman than for being black," she said. "Men are men."

The intersectionality of color bias and gender bias is clearly evident in pay gaps. As reported in "Equal Pay Day" for 2018, which is based on US Census data from 2016, black women earned $0.63 for every dollar earned by white men. Native American women earned $0.57 for every dollar, and Latina women earned $0.54. Meanwhile, white women and Asian American women earned $0.79 and $0.87, respectively.

We All See Color

Women of color also face frequent microaggressions at work, small insults based on internal biases that people deliver without realizing it. "When people see Latina, they automatically think certain things about me," leadership consultant Maggie Castro-Stevens told my team in an interview. People have assumed she came from a broken home, lived in the projects, has a spirited nature, grew up in Puerto Rico, and is overly emotional, none of which is true. White people often say she is being oversensitive when their stereotypical assumptions offend her, but Castro-Stevens said, "Don't blow it off as if it's not important; it's important to me. If it's important to me, it should be important to you. If we're working in a collaboration together, it's important to the outcome of the project." (See Chapters 6 and 7 for responses to the "You're too sensitive" criticism.)

I have learned so much from amazing women who make advancing other women their priority. Terra Renee is founder and president of the African American Women in Cinema foundation and film festival. She told me she received a call from a casting director who said Warner Brothers was shooting a motion picture in Manhattan and looking for a tall African-American woman for a role. When Renee went to the audition, she was shocked to find a thousand women like herself competing for a tiny role that might not even make it into the film, and decided to create roles and jobs for them.

Women everywhere, like Dr. Sheila Robinson, Terra Renee and Trudy Bourgeois, are working to inspire women to advance. At a Diversity Woman conference I heard women of color say they have to be twice as smart, be twice as educated, and work twice as hard, and they will still get only half of what they deserve. I learned that years of brutal discrimination taught these women to stick together and help each other. The women at those conferences know that their true power lies in working together.

Gender Identity and Sexual Orientation Bias

Ideas about gender identity and sexual orientation are changing fast, although society's rejection can still be strong. The idea of gender as binary (man or woman) is being replaced by gender as a universe that includes man, woman, non-binary, agender, transgender, and more. The understanding of sexual orientation is also expanding from straight and gay to include orientations like bisexual, pansexual, asexual, and more. The LGBTQ+ (lesbian, gay, bisexual, transgender, queer, and more) community is gaining mainstream acceptance and power, but our culture still inflicts punishments, including employment discrimination, verbal and physical harassment, and violence, on people who do not fit into what has been defined as "normal." Millennials strongly support equality initiatives that protect gender identity and sexual orientation, so acceptance will increase as younger generations take power. These facts from the Catalyst report "Lesbian, Gay, Bisexual, and Transgender Workplace Issues" demonstrate that progress in gender identity and sexual orientation equality in the US is far from complete:

- Seventy-two countries prohibit employment discrimination for sexual orientation.
- 71 percent of Americans support federal laws protecting LGBTQ people from discrimination in housing, public accommodations, and jobs, but:
    1. No federal law bars employment discrimination on the basis of sexual orientation or gender identity.
    2. In twenty-eight states you can be fired simply for being lesbian, bisexual, or gay.
    3. In thirty states you can be fired for being transgender.

As of 2017, 82 percent of *Fortune* 500 companies welcome LGBTQ+ employees and forbid discrimination based on gender identity and sexual orientation. However, most employees do not work at *Fortune* 500 companies, so most can still face institutional bias and bullying behaviors.

Gender Bias in STEM Careers

According to a University of California, Hastings study, 100 percent of women of color and 93 percent of white women in STEM jobs reported that they had experienced gender bias, reported Shalene Gupta in a *Fortune* article. This shows up clearly in speakers selected for conferences in these fields. At thirteen of the least egalitarian conferences "There were a total of just 11 women compared with 213 [men]... Seven conferences had no [women] speakers at all, and few conferences reached the 50 percent gender mark," wrote Apoorva Mandavilli in an article for *The Post and Courier*. Together, women are gathering and sharing data like these and increasing the pressure for change.

Age Bias

Barriers and competition arise between generations too. Youth and inexperience make new hires feel vulnerable and doubt themselves at work. Baby boomers flummoxed by constantly changing technologies may feel rusty and dusty. Every generation has its anxieties, and envy and jealousy divide us from each other. An older coworker may not realize that she is patronizing a younger woman by treating her like a daughter and offering unsolicited advice about her personal life, but this is bound to be resented. Let's instead treat each other with respect. Regardless of our age group, women are natural allies; each new generation of women has been raised to believe more fervently in equality than the one before it. Baby boomers are retiring at a rate of more than ten thousand a day, according to Glenn Kessler in *The Washington Post*, and by the year 2020 half of people working will be millennials born between 1981 and 2004.

> Regardless of our age group, women are natural allies; each new generation of women has been raised to believe more fervently in equality than the one before it.

Older generations fret about millennials' supposed failings and say unkind things about their abilities, but I know that's nonsense. The millennials I've worked with like to figure out their own processes, can multitask productively, like working in teams and solving problems collaboratively, and are poised for success because they are comfortable asking for what they want.

Older women often feel that their experience and wisdom are discounted and ignored by younger women. It's important to "really listen to the generations that have come before," said millennial Jamia Wilson in an interview with Senti Sojwal for *Feministing*. Wilson is also the first woman of color and the youngest woman ever to lead the Feminist Press as executive director. "I've always looked to older women to guide me," Wilson continued. "It's made me so much more committed to intergenerational feminism in a completely new way. I truly believe we all have to work together and that there is so much to learn from our foremothers who have dealt with so many things that we deal with now in a different form."

WORKING IN A BIAS-FREE WORKPLACE

In companies with inclusive environments "team members feel free to be themselves and bring their ideas forward," stated IBM's CMO Michelle Peluso in an interview with *Women 2.0*. "It's one thing to recruit diverse candidates into your team, but you need an inclusive environment to retain them and inspire people to contribute to their fullest potential. Leaders who do this best actively seek out different voices in a conversation, pull from different experiences, encourage openness about what's important to the different members of the team, and work to create an environment where people feel comfortable talking about their background, interests, and family lives."

> **" Don't listen to those who say YOU CAN'T. Listen to the voice inside yourself that says, I CAN. "**
>
> SHIRLEY CHISHOLM, second African-American woman in the New York State legislature and the first to run for a major party's presidential nomination

In an environment like this people will support and encourage each other. In order to become effective partners working for change, do people in different groups need to become best friends? Not at all. The point is that coming from a base of mutual respect will enable us to make common cause with members of other groups and work—together—on specific issues to make the workplace more equitable and flexible for everyone.

RECOGNIZING AND REDUCING THE IMPACT OF BIAS

I think our own internal biases have kept working women from believing that they have choices, that their partners or sons can be persuaded to do their share at home, or that they can work together with people different than themselves for equal pay and opportunity at work, even though most of us have seen examples proving that all these things are possible. Before we will agitate for such changes, we have to perceive that we have been disadvantaged by stereotype bias at work. Many hardworking women deny discrimination because admitting it would make them feel like victims, which would make them feel bad about themselves and their bosses or partners. Women want to get on with their lives and enjoy their relationships and the beauty of every day, so it's easier to decide that the spouse or the boss is fair than to start yet another fight. Plus, no one wants to start a fight they expect to lose. That's why Chapters 4, 7, and 10 suggest lots of ways to ask for what you want and strategies to help you get it.

Power of Collective Action

I'm betting every woman has encountered at least one of the challenges that Joan C. Williams and Rachel Dempsey outlined in their book, *What Works for Women at Work*:

- Continuously proving their credibility, expertise, and value to the organization
- Balancing act of maintaining the expected femininity, without being too strong or too weak
- Presumption that they will quit work to have a baby
- The "Tug of War" perspective among women who regard other women as threats

Although court cases have removed some barriers for women, change is increasingly occurring today without legal action. "Women can effectively band together to advance their cause, as the saga of Lawrence Summers illustrates," noted Rudman and Glick in *The Social Psychology of Gender*. "In 2005, Summers, then Harvard University's president, suggested that one reason women in science lag behind men might be innate gender differences." After women on faculty created publicity and a campaign to inform Summers about what really holds women back, Summers changed his tune, pledged to invest $50 million in improving Harvard University for women, expanded academic grants, and improved childcare. The outcry led to further national advancement for women scientists. "Thus," pointed out Rudman and Glick, "collective action is an important means by which women can combat sex discrimination in the workplace."

Women increasingly use social media today, and subcultures have developed their own, including Black Twitter, Feminist Twitter, and Asian American Twitter. People use these to raise issues that mainstream media ignore and to offer the perspectives of sources they consider more credible than national media celebrities. Increasingly conservative courts may be less receptive to suits than in the past, so finding ways to control the narrative and exert public pressure is valuable. "Many of the old tools that were used to break down barriers—anti-discrimination legislation and legal actions—can't protect women from subtle bias," noted Rosalind Barnett and Caryl Rivers in on the *Catalyst Blog*. "You can't sue because your boss thinks you're a bitch or because some guy got promoted on potential and you didn't."

Changing Expectations, Changing Behavior

Humans are amazingly able to change their behavior to match changing expectations. The social campaign to require seatbelt use is a great example. The first laws requiring people to wear seatbelts began in the 1980s; thirty years later almost 90 percent of people wear seatbelts, and accident death rates have fallen dramatically.

I think we're going to bring about huge advances for women in just a few years by working together. In pursuing difficult changes, remember "to stay open to opportunity and possibility," wrote consultant, author, and workplace drama expert Marlene Chism in an emailed newsletter. You shut yourself off from the possibility of change if you say, "I already know. Been there and done that. It'll never happen. Not worth it."

"It's easy to become cynical because of our past history," Chism wrote. "Where we gain perspective is when we use our wisdom while also realizing that we have the power to change internally. *And when we change internally* we experience huge shifts. The other person responds differently. There is an ease and flow. What was previously impossible now becomes possible. We see with new eyes...and we get new experiences."

Let's forget our false assumptions and heal the differences that keep us divided. There's plenty of blame for things that happened in the past, and we move not one inch closer to our goals when we focus our attention there. "All of us need to come out of our cocoons and share that the big blue earth belongs to more than me and my kind," said Castro-Stevens. "When we start recognizing that, and start thinking about others, then we can do things." Petty infighting and division keep women at the bottom. Let's focus instead on how we can work to create our bright future of equality together.

CHAPTER 3
DEFINE EACH OTHER AS LEADERS

" Anytime you have the power to influence something that is going to impact your community, society, and the world, you are a leader.**"**

DR. SHEILA ROBINSON, founder and publisher,
Diversity Woman Media

In this chapter we focus on the value women bring to work so you can watch for these abilities in the women all around you. Support them by applauding and helping to carry out their good ideas, and share stories about what makes them powerful and effective leaders. By highlighting their abilities, we position women as leaders eligible for top positions and encourage them to pursue those positions more confidently.

To define ourselves as leaders we must believe that we *are* leaders. It only takes the support of one person to help you believe in yourself. I see the faces of all the women in my life who supported me, and I was lucky to have many. Do you want to find a supporter? Try first offering support yourself. That starts the flow.

WOMEN'S STRENGTHS IMPROVE THE WORKPLACE
We often hear that women are nurturing, collaborative, empathetic, supportive, intuitive, and good at relationships, traits we express in

our socially conditioned roles. As we learned in the previous chapters, many men have those traits, too, but women have been rewarded for behaving that way much more often than men have. As "feminine" strengths, all these characteristics have been labeled "soft," low-power skills, and deemed more useful in support rather than leadership roles, causing some women to hide their feminine sides at work. Recent research, though, is showing that these skills are as useful at work as in life, and women are using these powerful strengths to build their business success. We don't have to wear severe suits to work anymore, and we don't have to pretend not to be women. Hooray!

Here are eleven characteristics often considered to be women's greatest strengths:

- **Emotional intelligence** is the capacity to notice, manage, and express emotions, and it's essential to being able to conduct interpersonal relationships wisely and with empathy. Women are accorded more freedom in our society to express a range of emotions than men are.
- **Empathy**, or the ability to understand and share other people's feelings, is important for a healthy workplace. The vast majority of employees value this trait, even though nearly half of CEOs say they have trouble expressing empathy.
- **Compassion** is a sympathetic consciousness of another person's distress combined with a desire to alleviate it. Most employees like to work for a boss who shows she cares. This makes it easier to cultivate positive relationships and boosts employee health, well-being, and retention, all of which help the bottom line.
- **Good communication skills** assist in delivering or exchanging information, which is essential to connecting with other people. Women excel at picking up nonverbal cues and using information to strengthen the bonds among people.
- **An ability to build relationships** affects the way people regard and behave toward each other. This is all about the way people connect, and women excel at connecting.

- **Multitasking skills** are essential at fast-paced companies, and women have them in spades, again possibly due to their many social responsibilities. Women multitask to increase their productivity and get ahead of their competition.
- **A tendency to collaborate,** or practice the art of working with someone else to produce something, is increasingly important in today's businesses. Women who care about the opinions and value the contributions of others are more likely to do it well.
- **A desire to mentor,** or engage in a professional relationship in which an experienced person assists someone less skilled to develop specific abilities or knowledge, is also valuable. Many women go out of their way to help others learn, which improves company atmosphere and productivity.
- **Passion**, a strong feeling of enthusiasm and excitement, drives women to excel and seek to improve their working worlds. Successful women know how to combine it with logic, creativity, and facts to avoid criticism for being too emotional.
- **Vulnerability** is often thought of as a weakness, but women who reveal their own vulnerability often inspire others to contribute their best. Asking for help allows coworkers to contribute their expertise, take pride in a project's success, and build a successful team. You don't have to have all the answers or skills yourself to be a successful leader. See Chapters 4 and 7 for specific scripts.
- **Endurance** is the ability to persist in the face of an unpleasant or difficult situation without giving way. Women have a boundless capacity to withstand wear and tear.

Although these are a few of women's traditional "feminine" skills, we actually have an abundance of abilities, such as persistence, problem solving, respect for others, the ability to learn from different perspectives, nurturing skills, spirituality, a tendency to support others, intuition, friendliness, expressiveness, vision of the future, the ability to empower others, listening skills, loyalty, trustworthiness, and authenticity. Each woman develops her own unique set of strengths, and we often use them in collaboration with others.

Our strengths translate readily into workplace skills, specifically long-term orientation, risk awareness, holistic decision making, a love of lifelong learning, and a sense of purpose, said Sallie Krawcheck, a former Wall Street analyst and CEO and cofounder of Ellevest, in her book *Own It: The Power of Women at Work*. Each woman has her own special package of strengths, whether traditionally feminine or not, that enable her to deliver benefits to companies like higher returns, lower risk, greater client focus, greater employee engagement, and greater innovation.

Focus On Value

Today's workforce is full of women who are highly skilled, experienced, and ambitious. They often dominate upper management, and our companies couldn't operate without them. These women need our support to see themselves as leaders, and to gain recognition of their abilities by their bosses, coworkers, and subordinates. We need to create a brand-new story. This is never easy because a huge image change always occurs outside your comfort zone. Change requires sweat and tears and failure. Hold hands with others to find the courage to begin again and again.

Encouraging and supporting each other is something anyone can do, whether they're entry level or CEO.

"Women financial bankers and women cashiers at McDonalds need to hold hands in solidarity," said millennial women's advocate Kaitlin Rattigan on Take The Lead's blog. "It needs to be both a top down and bottom up approach." Encouraging and supporting each other is something anyone can do, whether they're entry level or CEO. Low-wage workers are disproportionately women of color, and the divides between the affluent, the middle class, and the working poor are deep. By providing venues where socioeconomic classes work together and learn to respect each other, organizations like unions, political parties, churches, community social profit organizations, and women's philanthropic groups can provide opportunities for two-way mentoring and collaboration.

WHEN WOMEN WORK TOGETHER, CHANGE HAPPENS

Things are certainly better for women today than they were forty years ago in the 1970s. Then, a woman entering management or a profession as an executive or owner was a pioneer, often the sole woman in the company or even the entire industry in her town. She had no one to talk to because she was not allowed to join civic clubs like Rotary, Kiwanis, or the Jaycees, which were only for men.

A friend of mine told me this story about a group she joined in 1989. In 1976 a group of top-level women in Springfield, Missouri, a small Midwestern city, started a women's breakfast group, which grew into a lunch discussion group, and then became a club called simply "Network," which met twice every month for mutual support and problem solving. It was also a safe place where they could vent their frustration and rage at the ongoing condescension and sexism they encountered every day. Annoyed that there were so few women in positions of civic responsibility and authority, they set a goal of getting more women on area boards and commissions. They worked together with supportive men to challenge deep stereotypes of what a leader looks like. Committee members gathered information about open positions and systematically shared it with the group, recruited qualified women, encouraged them to apply for positions, and then supported and promoted their applications.

In those days women were taught that men wouldn't accept a woman's suggestions, so they invited men they knew to lunch and asked, "You're on such and such board. Can you think of a woman who would be a good board member?"

Network members were successful in placing scores of women on city and county governing bodies, including highly technical men's territory, like the airport and utility boards. Make no mistake; this was hard and uncomfortable for everyone, but the women were determined. A special task force succeeded repeatedly in placing women on the chamber of commerce board, including the first woman chair.

By 1987 the Supreme Court began hearing suits and ruling that men-only groups, like Rotary, would be required to admit women. Men-only social clubs were still allowed, but if the club was an engine of commerce, women could not be excluded.

Six years after those rulings, Network had disbanded. They no longer had time for a women-only club because women were now presidents of those former boys' clubs, running the show. They had changed forever the mindset in that community and in themselves, and today they still cherish indelible memories of the fun, sense of mission and accomplishment, and support they shared while making it happen.

Fast forward to 2017, when Rotary International acknowledged that only 20 percent of members internationally were women. But in Springfield, Missouri, more than 40 percent of Rotary's members were women. Women supporting other women made all the difference.

Remove Internal Barriers

It's not just preconceived notions in the minds of others that hold us back. Gloria Feldt teaches that our own internal biases may prevent us from acting with intention to match our ambition. By joining with each other, acting with courage, and developing a plan, Feldt said, a woman can realize her vision at work, at home, or in public life. When we help one another act strategically, we can redefine and establish ourselves in leadership positions.

Women on the rise take responsibility for building their own personal power rather than finding fault elsewhere. Women who are stuck often rob themselves of personal power, said workplace drama expert Marlene Chism, author of *No-Drama Leadership*.

Seven Ways We Rob Ourselves of Personal Power

1. Repeating the sad story about why it's so difficult
2. Excusing our own failure to act
3. Blaming others for our problems
4. Needing to feel good before taking action
5. Waiting for someone to agree
6. Refusing to let others feel discomfort
7. Using distractions to procrastinate

Source: Workplace drama expert Marlene Chism

"Taking responsibility is a lifetime journey," said Chism in an email. One way to take responsibility for your career is to intentionally define and position yourself as a leader. It's a fundamental identity shift that flies in the face of many gender biases. Of course, becoming a leader requires landing a leadership role, acquiring new skills, and developing your own style, but first and foremost we must *intend* to lead.

Women are still significantly underrepresented in corporations, according to the *Women in the Workplace 2017* report. "From the outset, fewer women than men are hired at the entry level, despite women being 57 percent of recent college graduates. At every subsequent step, the representation of women further declines, and women of color face an even more dramatic drop-off at senior levels. As a result, one in five C-suite leaders is a woman, and fewer than one in thirty is a woman of color." These numbers vary only a little each year.

Learn to Ask
Learning to ask is like flexing a muscle, so the more you do it, the easier it becomes. Sadly, what you deserve will not automatically come

to you. It is only in advocating for yourself that you will receive what you deserve. "I used to believe that if I worked hard and put my head down, someone would notice how much value I created," said Caroline Ghosn, founder and CEO of Levo, who works to help millennials navigate the workplace, in an article in *Well+Good*. "I thought talking about it was crass, or conceited. I was dead wrong. You can't count on anyone looking out for you—you need to speak up to succeed."

Although companies say they realize they need to change and claim that their commitment to gender diversity is high, the gender wage gap and number of women in leadership have barely budged in decades. Is it some kind of plot perpetrated by men against women? I don't think so, and I don't see how it would help to approach the situation from that perspective anyway.

JUDGMENTS THAT HOLD WOMEN BACK

I want to briefly address some of the specific penalties and hazards that keep women from advancing so you can recognize when these judgments are being made. Once we start to see it, we can support each other by speaking up and provide a more accurate view of women's abilities. Chapter 4 offers scripts and techniques you can use. It's worth understanding the dynamics of likability, credibility, assertiveness, parenthood, modesty, and negotiation so you won't take the discrimination personally. It's not you—it's them.

Likability Challenge

All women walk a tightrope between being seen as competent and being well liked, and it's very hard for women to win at both. "As I began to climb the ladder," wrote the first woman secretary of state, Madeleine Albright, in her memoir, *Madam Secretary*, "I had to cope with the different vocabularies used to describe similar qualities in men (confident, take-charge, committed) and women (bossy, aggressive, emotional)." She also noticed that men were heard and acknowledged even when they behaved in ways that would have been dismissed if they had been women.

"Women face a double standard that men don't," Sheryl Sandberg wrote in *People* magazine. "Men are expected to be assertive and confident, while women are expected to be nurturing and collaborative. When women take the lead and assert ourselves, we go against expectations—and often face pushback from men and women." Sandberg's concern that assertive girls are labeled harsh, abrasive, and bossy prompted her "Ban Bossy" campaign.

The more accomplished a woman is, the more likely she'll be subject to the likability penalty encountered by Ann Hopkins and Shelley Weinstock. Powerful women who step outside of gender stereotypes are disliked and seen as bitches. This is a real problem because people who are disliked are less likely to advance than those who are likable.

> The more accomplished a woman is, the more likely she'll be subject to the likability penalty.

Political people are no exception. Michelle Obama worked to soften her image during the 2008 presidential campaign to avoid being branded as an "angry black woman." Hillary Clinton is thought to have lost her own presidential bid because she was not likable. The fact that she was smart, articulate, and politically proficient put her outside accepted feminine norms. While the men who opposed her were allowed to speak authoritatively and raise their voices to make a point on issues they were passionate about, Valentina Zarya wrote in *Fortune* that Hillary was told by male journalists that she needed to "smile more."

Credibility Challenge

Because our leaders have always been men, people feel deeply conflicted about women who exercise authority and wonder whether they should lead at all. Men's credibility is often assumed, and many get by with a "believe me" approach. In contrast, women are rarely taken at their word and instead have to prove, document, and justify themselves again and again. The bias against believing women was deeply ingrained, wrote Soraya Chemaly, award-winning media critic and director of the Women's Media Center Speech Project. "No one says, 'You can't trust women,' but distrust them we do. College students surveyed revealed that they think up to 50% of their female peers lie when they accuse someone of rape, despite wide-scale evidence and multi-country studies that show the incidence of false rape reports to be in the 2% to 8% range, pretty much the same as false claims for other crimes." Chemaly reports that women's credibility is questioned every day: at work when they are not heard, in courts when their testimony is disbelieved, by law enforcement when their complaints are ignored, in doctors' offices when their symptoms are denied, and in our political processes when men make rules that disregard the needs women have clearly expressed.

In her *Boston Globe* review of Leigh Gilmore's *Tainted Witness: Why We Doubt What Women Say About Their Lives*, Kate Tuttle wrote that women's stories have been seen as dangerous to all systems in which men control power. "They're threatening to institutions, including the church, government, other interests," said Gilmore. "To keep women's stories from taking root, people in power, generally men, go straight at the credibility of the woman."

We can counteract this penalty by supporting each other and calling out this bias when we see it. Women can prevail by staying calm, getting our facts in order, and using them to back up what we say.

Assertiveness Challenge

It's hard to lead if you can't assert yourself, and women pay a greater price than men for being judged as forceful. This is true even for someone like actress Jennifer Lawrence, star of the *The Hunger Games*, who dared to speak her mind in a blunt, no-nonsense way at work. The man she was working with recoiled, saying, "Whoa! We're all on the same team here!" as if she were really crossing a line. "I'm over trying to find the 'adorable' way to state my opinion," she wrote in an essay for *Lenny Letter*. "I don't think I've ever worked for a man in charge who spent time contemplating what angle he should use to have his voice heard. It's just heard."

As Kathy Caprino reported in *Forbes*, a woman is perceived as 35 percent less competent when she is judged as being "forceful," compared to a 22 percent drop for a forceful man. Perceived worth also dropped, although assertive women lost more than twice as much value as men. This type of sexism is difficult to address because people are usually not aware of their biases and will deny that they have them. Discouragingly, women are particularly penalized for explicit verbal behavior, such as negotiating for more pay. Compensation is indeed risky territory for women.

The assertiveness penalty taints employee evaluations, too, as linguist Kieran Snyder reported in *Fortune*. She examined 248 evaluations from businesses, including large tech companies, looking at gender differences without regard to race or ethnicity. She found that it wasn't performance that drew negative feedback as much as it was personality: "Words like *bossy*, *abrasive*, *strident*, and *aggressive* are used to describe women's behaviors when they lead; words like *emotional* and *irrational* describe their behaviors when they object. All of these words show up at least twice in the women's review text I reviewed, some much more often." The word *abrasive* never appeared in men's reviews but occurred seventeen times in evaluations of thirteen different women.

> **If they don't give you a seat at the table, bring a folding chair.**
>
> SHIRLEY CHISHOLM, second Africa-American woman in the New York State legislature and the first to run for a major party's presidential nomination

Parenthood Challenge

For decades it's been known that women with children receive lower pay and fewer promotions than women without children, according to the National Partnership for Women & Families. Low-wage mothers with children under six experience a wage penalty five times as great as that of higher-paid women with young children, wrote sociology professor Michelle Budig, who has studied the parenthood pay gap. I've experienced that myself. When I asked for a raise, my employer told me my pay did not need to be higher because I was married and had children. Some evidence shows that devoted fathers who place a high priority on their families are penalized as well.

Women are also penalized for the fact that they could—regardless of whether they will—bear children. Case in point, a 2008 *Scotsman* article titled "Pregnancy Risk Puts Employers Off Women" reported on a survey that found that more than half of bosses would use a woman's age and marital status to try to estimate the likelihood of her becoming pregnant. Even though they could not legally ask for that information, they still used it in their decisions for hiring and promotions.

Several high-profile women have recently shone light on these issues. Senator Tammy Duckworth made history as the first-ever US senator to give birth while in office, and for changing Senate rules to allow her to bring her infant to the floor so she could breastfeed and not miss a vote. Pointing out that women can be both mothers and professionals, Senator Duckworth used her own pregnancy to further very public discussions on pregnancy, employment, and paid family leave. In fact, the US is the only industrialized country not to offer paid maternity leave. In her article on *Mic*, "It's Not the 'Confidence Gap'—Here's What's Really Holding Women Back," Elizabeth Plank wrote, "Approximately half of mothers in the US workforce don't receive any paid leave, and many of them are forced by their employers to leave work early in their pregnancy without remuneration." This puts many women at a terrible disadvantage, and the lack of family-friendly policies keeps many of them out of the workplace for years.

Removing the parenthood penalty and creating a workplace that allows women to balance career and family responsibilities is key. As it stands right now, even if she can get her foot in the door, a sick child or family emergency can wreak havoc on a woman's road to advancement or even cost her the job.

Removing the parenthood penalty and creating a workplace that allows women to balance career and family responsibilities is key.

New Zealand's prime minister, Jacinda Ardern, also got conversations started when she announced that she was pregnant with her first child. Samantha Schmidt reported in *The Washington Post* that just hours after she won the election in 2017 two television hosts asked about her plans for a family, a question I doubt has ever been asked of a man. In fact, one of the hosts asked her specifically whether it was *permissible* for a nation's prime minister to take maternity leave while in office. "It is totally unacceptable in 2017 to say that women should have to answer that question in the workplace," Ardern fired back. Senator Duckworth and Prime Minister Ardern are in the vanguard of women who refuse to pretend they are not women in order to lead. Kelda Roys, a Democratic candidate in Wisconsin's 2018 gubernatorial race, actually nursed her infant in a campaign ad about her work to ban Bisphenol A in baby bottles and sippy cups in the state. Times are changing indeed, and by supporting each other, women can accelerate these changes.

Modesty Challenge
Women need to support each other in defining ourselves as leaders because we are working against thousands of years of cultural conditioning. From early on girls are raised to be seen, not heard, modest not bragging. Having opinions or acknowledging that you're good at something can draw ridicule and harassment, often from your own peers, and the whispers can create anxiety.

Girls Learn to Hide Themselves in Childhood

Girls learn in earliest elementary school to hide their accomplishments to avoid being picked on. Young girls in every community are harassed for their good looks, bad looks, athletic abilities or lack thereof, good grades, bad grades, and everything in between. Throughout school girls learn that something as simple as a hairstyle or fashion choice can cause celebration, scorn, or racial discrimination, and it's often impossible for them to predict which. Girls can be exceptionally vicious toward one another in their formative years (boys can, too, but in different ways). We talk more about this in Chapter 5.

"Girls are socialized to be more modest than boys and it is more acceptable for boys to talk about themselves and their achievements," according to Australian psychologist Prue Laurence, quoted in a *Daily Life* article. When a woman brags, she violates gender expectations and, of course, draws punishment at work as in the schoolyard. This inevitably causes women to avoid claiming credit for their accomplishments. Congratulate a woman for a job well done and you will likely hear something along the lines of, "It was nothing." This is where support and praise from other women help us define ourselves as leaders.

Avoid Wounding the Male Ego

The threat of judgment from a peer group is real, and now with social media it can come in an instant from the world at large. If the judgment, taunts, and slights aren't enough to stop a woman in her tracks, the threat of the single life might be. For generations women have been taught to hide their light to avoid making men feel inadequate, a crucial life skill practiced by the majority of women who want to marry and make a life with a man. Women of previous generations would caution their teenage daughters against wounding the "fragile male ego." I wish that was no longer the case, but that dynamic persists with women taking responsibility for men's emotions.

Big Decision: Career Success or Marriage?

Young, professional women MBA candidates minimize their accomplishments and ambitions, but only if they're single, wrote Lauren Weber in a January 2017 article in *The Wall Street Journal*. She reported on a new study revealing that men MBA candidates prefer as partners women who are less ambitious and less educated than they are, that marital satisfaction is lower and divorce more likely when a woman out-earns her husband, and that promotions increase the chance of divorce for women but not men. That profile would fit with many men's gender expectations, and the study does indicate that a woman who is interested in snagging one of those men MBA candidates faces a tough choice: boldly pursue her ambitions and remain single or downplay her hopes and successes as a way to find a mate.

The problem is that neither approach is appealing for most women. However, other studies point out that women who partner with men who believe in equality for women are more satisfied and have more sex than those who marry traditional men. Also, women have proven that they can support themselves, and the number of them who out-earn their husbands is on the rise.

Hiding Your Feminism

Traditional men do feel threatened by strong women, though. Radio personality Rush Limbaugh in 1992 drove a stake into the heart of the word *feminist* by coining the term *feminazi* and defining feminism as bad for men. This bad rap quickly overshadowed the true definition, a belief in equal rights for women. Women recoiled in fear that others might think they were failing at their primary role—supporting men. I'm sure some feminists were angry and unpleasant, and men who did not get the deference they believed they deserved felt abused and resentful. They pushed back against women's equality, and even today the fear of being thought unfeminine, an unnatural woman, and therefore unable to attract and keep a man prevents many women from sticking up for themselves or each other.

Owning Women's Leadership Strengths

I think it's a positive sign that increasing numbers of women, especially Generation X and millennials, refuse to downplay what they can do. Many social penalties aim to keep "women from competing on an equal footing for prestigious, male-dominated occupations," Rudman and Glick wrote. There is evidence, however, that a woman who skillfully blends her strengths in relationships and collaboration with her assertive traits can minimize any negative backlash. In fact, the authors say, "research on leadership style suggests that doing so results in being a more effective leader."

We Need to Toot Our Horns

A man will proudly tell you his golf handicap and how much money he makes and who he knows. A woman can be a Supreme Court justice and never reveal her importance. Men blow their whistles, and women need to toot their horns. We can truly help each other celebrate our accomplishments, step confidently into our next projects, and define ourselves as leaders. When we shine light on each other's successes and celebrate one another's victories, we get increased credibility and credit for our accomplishments *without* paying a bragging penalty. This support is crucial to helping women advance.

Negotiation Challenge

In their 2003 book *Women Don't Ask*, Carnegie Mellon professors Linda Babcock and Sara Laschever concluded that men asked for raises and promotions four times more often than women did. That may have been true then, but it's different now. A 2016 study conducted by Andrew Oswald and others from London's Cass Business School, the University of Warwick, and the University of Wisconsin tested the idea that women are paid less because they ask less and found that it isn't true at all. Like a similar LeanIn study, researchers found that women ask every bit as often as men but that men get what they're asking for about 25 percent more often than women do.

"Having seen these findings, I think we have to accept that there is some element of pure discrimination against women," stated Oswald. We knew that, right?

It is reasonable, then, for women to feel apprehensive about tough negotiating. "Women worry that pushing for more money will damage their image," reported Ashley Milne-Tyte on NPR's *Planet Money.* "Research shows they're right to be concerned: Both male and female managers are less likely to want to work with women who negotiate during a job interview."

This tough negotiator penalty is real. "In repeated studies, the social cost of negotiating for higher pay has been found to be greater for women than it is for men," reported Hannah Riley Bowles in *Harvard Business Review.* Ask your boss for more money and risk being seen as ungrateful and pushy; don't ask for more and you'll be paid less for the rest of your career.

Women are increasingly willing to risk being thought unladylike, though. One woman I know went to her library reference section and found a publication that listed average salaries by state for men and women. She based her salary request on the average in her field for men, which was thousands higher. "I'm not average," she said calmly, keeping a neutral tone and providing a photocopy of the data. The decision went up all levels of the organization to the very top because no woman had ever asked for that much, but in the end she got what she asked for.

WOMEN LEADERS WORK TO HELP EACH OTHER

In her book *Black Women's Lives,* Kristal Zook wrote about Sarah White, a black woman and laborer at a catfish plant who, in 1990, led the largest strike of black workers (most of them women) in Mississippi history. In a telephone conversation, Zook said this caused the plant's owners, who included former slave-owning families, to push back *hard,* but White persevered to become a union leader at the plant and continued to support her coworkers. The union asked White to give speeches, but when Zook asked if they were paying her for it, White explained that she couldn't bring herself to ask for money for talking. Despite all her struggle and sacrifice, she still didn't feel worthy of asking.

Today, women make up about half of union membership and continue to fill some of the leadership positions, but with the decreasing power of traditional unions, alt-labor groups and worker centers are on the rise to represent workers' interests. Many of today's largest new worker-advocate groups are run by women. Following are some of the ways that women help each other when they lead.

Equal Leadership Creates Successful Companies

Recent large studies have focused on white-collar industries and the results are crystal clear: companies and organizations that invest in gender equality by promoting women to positions of leadership are more successful, period. McKinsey & Company's research reported by Vivian Hunt and her coauthors supports this. More diversity in leadership leads to better overall performance and higher profits. "Gender equality is not a female issue," wrote Shelley Zalis, chief executive and founder of The Girls' Lounge in a 2017 *Forbes* article. "It's a social and economic issue."

When women help define each other as leaders and emphasize the value women deliver, more women will be able to advance into leadership. Use facts and figures like these when you build the case for advancing women into leadership at your company (you'll find links to the studies in the Selected Bibliography):

- **Increased profit:** *Fortune* 500 companies with the highest representation of women board directors achieved markedly better results, according to a 2007 Catalyst report. They logged 53 percent higher return on equity, 42 percent higher profit on sales, and 66 percent higher return on invested capital. Companies in the top quartile for gender diversity are 15 percent more likely to financially outperform their counterparts in the lower quartile, according to McKinsey & Company, and firms with gender-balanced executive committees had a 56 percent higher operating profit than companies whose committees had only men. Companies with at least 30 percent women in senior management had a 15 percent higher net revenue margin than companies with no women in senior management, reported Marcus Noland, Tyler Moran, and Barbara Kotschwar on the Peterson Institute for International Economics's global study. Now that's impressive!

- **Increased revenue:** MIT researchers found that a more even gender split not only leads to happier, more productive employees, but it can also increase revenue by 41 percent, reported Peter Dizikes. Similarly, a Sodexo report showed 42 percent better profit margins and 53 percent higher average shareholder returns when one-third of the board members were women as compared to boards with no women, according to Lisa Anderson in a Thomson Reuters Foundation News article.

- **Better recruitment and retention:** McKinsey & Company found that companies with more balanced leadership do a better job recruiting and retaining talented workers, leading to reduced costs for replacing top executives.

- **Advancement of women:** Companies that want to profit from having sharp women at the top might take note: where women and men believed that progress was being made toward gender diversity, 85 percent of women were seeking top spots. At companies not seen as moving toward gender diversity, just 66 percent of women reported such ambitions, according to an infographic in a report by Katie Abouzahr and others for the Boston Consulting Group, "Dispelling the Myths of the Gender 'Ambition Gap.'"

- **More effective problem solving:** More women in the workplace generally equals better problem solving. Why? According to Development Dimensions International's "Ready-Now Leaders" report, "encouraging gender diversity in your leadership pool means greater diversity of thought, which, in turn, leads to improved problem solving and greater business benefits."

Racial and Ethnic Diversity Boosts Company Returns

McKinsey & Company's "Diversity Matters" report looked at 366 public companies in Canada, Latin America, the United Kingdom, and the United States. It found that those in the top 25 percent for gender diversity were 15 percent more likely to have financial returns above industry medians, and those who ranked high in terms of racial and ethnic diversity were 35 percent more likely to experience the same. Researchers also found that racial and ethnic diversity had a stronger impact than gender diversity on financial performance in the US. Unfortunately, these studies did not specifically address the contributions of women of color, although one might assume some were represented in the workforces studied. Despite the demonstrated benefits, researchers also found that companies were not embracing diversity in their top roles. The McKinsey report further stated that a whopping 78 percent of UK companies had senior-leadership teams that failed to reflect the composition of the labor force. This figure, however, actually put them far ahead of Brazil (91 percent not diverse) and the US (97 percent not diverse).

Just as women leaders have an impact on a company's bottom line, they also contribute heavily to their communities. ManpowerGroup suggests a strong correlation between the countries that are the most successful at closing the gender gap and those that are the most economically competitive. The reality is that the barriers preventing a woman's full participation in the workforce also act as brakes on the national economy, stifling its ability to grow. "The United States could add up to $4.3 trillion in annual GDP in 2025 if women attain full gender equality," wrote Kweilin Ellingrud and other analysts at McKinsey & Company. The McKinsey report notes that every US state and city could add at least 5 percent to their GDP by capitalizing on the economic potential of women; half of states could grow GDP by more than 10 percent; and the fifty largest cities could increase GDP by as much as 13 percent.

Getting Credit for Accomplishments

Research from MIT showed that the basis for the most successful teams in business was not the IQs of the members of the team, according to women's business expert Sharon Hadary; it was *whether or not they had women on the team*. Yet women often lack the confidence to take the credit. Hadary told me about a woman manager who was complimented by a senior VP for the success of a project. She responded, "Oh, it wasn't me; it was my team, but thank you." It's hard for a woman to acknowledge that without her leadership her team would not have been successful. This is another tightrope for women because appearing to brag will draw criticism. It's different when another person touts your success, though, so this is a perfect opportunity for women to support other women.

Plenty of Room at the Top

It's no longer the situation of a few decades ago when women felt they had to bite and scratch their way up because there was room at the top for only one token woman. Today, there is room for many, and those of us who reach the top can continue to work to make space for all of us. "Not enough pie" was a phrase used in the past to define women's competitiveness with each other. Today, though, women's leadership is an "infinite pie," said Gloria Feldt. In my podcast interview with her she said some people have been surprised that she freely shares her prizewinning recipe for chocolate marble cheesecake, but in her view it's not a competitive win-lose proposition. She loves to share the recipe because she believes, "The more there is, the more there is. The pie just keeps getting bigger."

Believe in Abundance

In this time of tremendous opportunity I'm convinced that it's better to focus on what women have accomplished rather than our roadblocks. We've been telling the stories of scarcity for so long, explained filmmaker Tiffany Shlain, that it has blinded us to the abundance of all we have accomplished. Having an attitude of scarcity creates lots of problems, not the least being that people want to align with a winner, not a whiner. In her film *50/50: Rethinking the Past, Present & Future of Women + Power*, Shlain noted that more than 300 studies have shown that elevating women to power in business, politics, and culture makes it better for everyone. The evidence is on our side, so how do we get to the world we want to see?

See Ourselves As Worthy of Leadership

We need to see ourselves as able to have and worthy of having equal power because, as Feldt has taught, a primary person keeping a woman from parity today is herself. Our internal biases regarding what a woman ought to be keep us from aspiring to leadership. The doors of opportunity are open, though, and we have already seen a first woman in almost every role, although too few women have joined them. Women who believe ourselves strong and capable can organize and work together with others, as Sarah White did, to insist on more equal opportunity and pay.

Make Others See Our Potential

One way that women can advance in the ranks is by seeing and embracing women's potential as leaders. That means that even if a woman hasn't yet demonstrated a particular skill, you believe she will master it. Joanna L. Krotz told me during our interview that women are hired for the proven experience on their résumé, but men are hired for the potential of what they might do. On the *Catalyst Blog* in 2014 Rosalind Barnett and Caryl Rivers agreed that it's definitely bias that causes hotshot young men to move up the ladder ahead of their more seasoned women peers. "Women have to prove themselves over and over and constantly fight the stereotype that they don't have what it takes to be real leaders," they stated. "Even in female-dominated fields, men get on the 'Glass Escalator' and rise faster and higher than their equally qualified women colleagues."

Counteract This Bias: Think Manager, Think Man

This ingrained bias is mostly unconscious, possibly intentional, but real. The messages in our media, on news shows, and in the marketplace feed our biases and fears daily. This is extremely detrimental to women's careers, but if we become aware of it, we can counteract it. Just as venture capitalists want to loan start-up money to people like themselves—white men—Krotz said that corporate managers who are men tend to reward and promote people like themselves—white men. It's natural for a man who has succeeded by following a certain trajectory to see the same potential in other men.

This is the "think manager, think man" approach, reported Raina Brands in *The Guardian.* "When we are asked to evaluate someone's leadership potential, we subconsciously compare them to our expectations." When our expectations are confirmed, we tend to project lots of other leadership qualities and behaviors onto the person, *even if that person has never exhibited them.* Because our culture has taught us that leadership is a masculine trait, we tend to evaluate men as a good fit. Hiring managers in many institutions just don't think about hiring more women or that women might be having trouble coming up through the ranks. It doesn't occur to them. I recently had a conversation with the CEO of a trust company where I serve as a director. I suggested that we add more women, but the candidates who had been recommended by the other board members were almost exclusively male. We talk in Chapter 4 about how to build a case for appointing more women.

Help Women See Their Own Potential to Lead

It's unfortunate but inevitable that women adopt these unconscious biases as well, and that it prevents them from seeing their own potential. Having supportive women around makes all the difference, however. A group of millennials described how hard they worked to encourage a coworker to seek a promotion because she doubted herself and agonized even though her boss had urged her to apply. With her coworkers' support the young woman did apply, and of course, she got the job. It takes only one woman to support and encourage another woman. Picture the faces of those who helped you along the way. You owe it to them—and to yourself—to do the same.

By recognizing the potential in ourselves and other women leaders, we can broaden the concept of leadership and make opportunities more available to even more talented leaders who may be left out because of their race, ethnicity, or sexual orientation. Culture used to change glacially, but in the current century we have seen issues like marriage equality and marijuana legalization progress rapidly from unthinkable to inevitable. I see that happening with women's equality at work too.

I often speak to groups, and once women confess their aspirations for leadership and making a difference, pure joy fills the room. When I say we are building a community of like-minded women, a sisterhood, women around me are exhilarated. When I say they are all leading women, I love to see their smiles and joy as they look around and say, "Yes! We are!" This is a movement I'm thrilled to help pioneer. Please join me. Let's be pioneers together, support and amplify one another, and create and believe in our own ability to lead. Together, by supporting other women in the workplace, we can *all* gain an equal opportunity to earn, lead, and advance.

CHAPTER 4

WHAT YOU CAN SAY AND DO

> " We sit in the shade of trees we did not plant
> We drink from wells we did not dig
> We profit from persons we did not know
> This is as it should be.
> Together we are more than any one person could be. "

REV. PETER RAIBLE, Unitarian leader

Women have always used their strengths to raise their families, safeguard their communities, and grow successful businesses, but we have not usually thought of ourselves as leaders. Today, though, we have countless opportunities to work together, support each other, and redefine our leadership potential. We can overcome gender limitations caused by bias and step into our power to help each other advance. This chapter offers actions for using your strengths to propel yourself forward and bring other women with you. Review these techniques with women in your community, make your plans together, and you will succeed. The scenarios and scripts in this chapter can be modified to fit a wide variety of situations.

BUILD YOUR "POWER TO"

We all have inner power, although we may not be aware of it and might have been actively discouraged from using it. By working together, we can help each other overcome any tendency to undercut other women. As Regina Huber, a certified leadership ambassador for Take The Lead, Inc., said, "Don't shut her down when she reaches for power. Support and encourage her."

Example: Emily found herself in a new department of fifty overachievers and knew that to advance she had to find an empty niche. Everyone in the department could request her services, but if she waited for that to happen, she might never get the opportunity she wanted. Instead, she took the initiative to work together proactively with her fellow employees, and:

1. Asked her coworkers about their projects and what they hoped to achieve
2. Strategized how to help them, suggested a plan, and listened to their input
3. Refined her ideas for improving each coworker's outcome

Her manager welcomed her ideas because they made him and his department more successful. By taking on more responsibility and making more efficient use of her services, Emily created a larger role in the department. Because she took the time to connect with her coworkers in helpful ways, all of them supported her efforts.

"Understand that there are no limitations to what you're capable of," Ashten Fizer said in an interview for *Blavity*. "If you think it, you can be it. All you have to do is get up and do it. No, seriously, just go do it! Don't stand in your own way!"

Advocate for Yourself

Women need to build up their leadership styles and unabashedly advocate for themselves, said women's business expert Sharon Hadary in our podcast interview. We need to demonstrate the ways we bring value to the company. Men who come in to ask for a promotion say, "Here are all the things I did in my last job. I increased productivity by X percent, I increased profitability by Y percent, and if you give me this job, I will increase sales by XY percent." When women come to me and ask for a promotion, they say, "I did everything you asked of me and I did it well. I deserve the promotion." That's not effective. Instead women need to develop a business case for their new role based on real numbers that represent value to the company.

Example: Angela wanted to move from hotel marketing into management.

1. She positioned herself by increasing her connections with other employees, volunteering to lead a team, and organizing a campaign to get more off-season tour groups into the hotel.
2. She planned a strategy, implemented it, and recorded her results.
3. She advocated for herself and stated her case: "As team leader, I oversaw research into an untapped demographic, developed group rates they could afford, and partnered with tour companies to increase their non-peak offerings. Our overall occupancy increased last year by X percent and our profitability by Y percent."
4. She quantified the value she would deliver: "I have a plan for increasing sales to other untapped demographics that should increase convention occupancy by X percent and restaurant business by Y percent."
5. She asked for what she wanted: "I want to become a manager because it will enable me to achieve these results for the company."

Show You Can Handle More Responsibility

Patty is a bank teller who wants a more responsible customer service role, but her manager can't visualize her in that position. She wants to become a personal banker, sit at the welcome desk, and help open accounts. Patty strategizes ways to distance herself from her stuck position.

1. She asks her supervisor for what she wants: "When I'm not busy, may I relieve Janet at the front desk when she needs a break?"
2. She develops her business case: "I'm familiar with all the account types and have already been helping clients when Janet's busy or there's no one to relieve her."
3. She outlines the benefits to the company: "I can help create a better experience for our customers by going up front during those times."
4. She increased her mobility so that she was seen in multiple areas of the bank. When a higher-ranking position opens up, she will be ready to move again.

Get a Boss to Sponsor You for a Promotion

Camryn, like many millennials, expected to work for a boss who would advocate for her. By acting strategically, she made that happen.

- She developed the relationship by volunteering to do things that were challenging or tedious for her boss.
- She took on bigger assignments and asked for advice on improving her usefulness to the company.
- She took every opportunity to work with others, invested in new training, and earned the respect of her coworkers.
- She watched for a new opening, then asked her boss to support her application.

When a position opened up, her boss sponsored her.

HOW TO ADVOCATE FOR OTHERS

Women are stepping forward to support others like never before. Helping other women advance is one of the best ways to support each other and also help ourselves. Try these techniques to help women earn more and advance, no matter where we work.

Amplify Each Other

Amplification is a technique that can be used to support others for various purposes. In one office women were far outnumbered by men, but they decided to stick together. They strategized to support one another, help each other get comfortable with their power, and claim the roles they wanted. When one woman's idea was "bropriated" (her idea was ignored, but moments later it was applauded when a man said the same thing), they agreed to consistently bring attention and credit back to the woman who made the original suggestion. It worked!

Examples of What You Can Say:

- "George, I'm glad you like Marie's idea. Marie, could you please give us a few more data points on that?"
- "Sounds like we all agree with Louise, who made that suggestion a few minutes ago."
- "Louise, how does Bob's idea build on yours?"
- "Sally and Belinda did a good job on that research. Can we hear from them how they viewed the results?"

You don't have to be the group leader to amplify another woman's ideas. Communication dynamics are usually fluid, so stay alert to ways that you can amplify women's voices. Pre-planning can help, and you probably already know the likely bropriators in your group.

Be friendly and polite, but do speak up. Women in any work group can gain this kind of power when they support one another. The #MeToo movement and The Women's March are examples of this on a mass scale. Insist on being heard and help each other tell your stories.

HELP OTHERS OVERCOME SELF-DOUBT

When women face bias, stereotyping, and double standards, their self-confidence can suffer. This self-doubt is especially noticeable when women think about trying for a new job or responsibilities.

You can help a woman overcome her belief that she has to be perfect to even apply, or that she's not qualified to do a job if she hasn't had experience in everything it requires. Remind her that every employer expects to do on-the-job-training, and help her practice selling her ability to quickly learn the job.

- Convince each other that good enough is okay.
- Learn to practice "good bragging" even if it violates stereotypes. Help each other put into words the value for the company that your experience and actions delivered. Use real numbers.
- Practice building each other up to amplify self-love, self-respect, self-care, and self-empowerment.
- Encourage each other to take risks. Failing is better than not trying at all. If one of you fails, have a brief pity party, then learn from it, and move on. Build on that experience the next time you try something new.

Form Your Own Support Group

A friend of mine treasures her small entrepreneurial support group. Years ago a woman in her professional association invited three other members to meet monthly for breakfast. All four occupied different business niches and knew each other but were not close. They soon developed trust, found that they could bring any challenge to the group, and relied on the problem solving assistance they always received. Fifteen years later their businesses are thriving, and when they meet quarterly for happy hour, they are more likely to talk about their kids and grandkids than business problems.

Women have always come together in support groups, and the best part of women connecting with women is that you will have fun while you get important things done. Remember my motto: put five women in a room, and they will develop a plan, solve a problem, and chart a course to a positive result. Find or create a support system of peers united by something you're passionate about. Tend and befriend other women who share that passion and experience the amazing joy of working with like-minded women.

Eight Ways Women Can Help Women Advance

The following eight action steps were developed by Alliance, a group of powerful professional women working in the Midwest in the 1990s. It was an organization of organizations, conceived as a kind of super-network with members from fifteen area and national women's clubs. These were their top recommendations to help women advance:

1. Help others help you through networking and mentorships.
2. Ask for feedback on your strengths and how to maximize them.
3. Ask for feedback on your weaknesses and how to minimize them.
4. Ask for feedback on how you conduct yourself with supervisors and colleagues outside of your specific job.
5. Tell each other about new opportunities.
6. Share opportunities for training in your industry.
7. Suggest training opportunities to your employer and bring in new learning.
8. Share information inside and outside of your company about pay ranges for similar jobs and in your market.

BUILD STRATEGIC RELATIONSHIPS VIA NETWORKING

I think women's most formidable strength is building relationships. This is what networking is really about, not just connecting on LinkedIn, trading cards, or getting business leads. You can't predict when someone you know might make a connection to help you in your career or your life, or when you might help someone else with a referral. The depth and breadth of your network also build a personal and professional safety net, and the connections themselves can bring great joy and satisfaction.

Getting Started

Not everyone is born knowing how to network effectively, but it is a skill that can be learned with practice. If you usually communicate digitally, you may struggle to overcome shyness, but stick with it and you'll learn to make face-to-face business connections. Plan to make a positive impression and leave people with a desire to see more of you. If the idea of networking alone terrifies you, practice by looking for connections in your daily life.

- Ask questions and learn about people you meet at work, in your community, and during social activities.
- Learn tactics (online or in books) for remembering names and relating those to their jobs, where you met them, and what impressed you.

When you can meet new people without feeling panicky, plan your strategy with a woman friend.

- Attend networking events with a colleague or friend. It's much more fun and a great way for women to support each other. Introduce each other around and say nice things about everyone. For example, "I'd like to introduce my friend and coworker Angela, who came up with an idea that raised our productivity by 10 percent last quarter."
- Share information with others to make helpful connections. For example, tell Sandra (who needs new health insurance) about Melissa's independent insurance agency.
- Pay special attention to women who are natural "connectors" and get to know them. Make sure they know what abilities you bring to their network. Always share your thoughts and ideas briefly after listening to others. This shows confidence and generosity and makes you stand out, so toot your horn.
- Learn about their other connections that might benefit you and ask for introductions.

- Reciprocate and offer introductions to people who might enlarge their network. Say one positive and interesting thing about each person you're introducing (extra points if you can make a connection between the two of them!), giving them somewhere to go in conversation. For example: "Maria, this is Tammy, who left SmithCo. just before you were hired. Tammy opened the Paris office in their international branch. Maria stayed at an Airbnb in Paris last year and had an interesting experience."

Network with a Purpose

Remember that networking isn't just about business development. While pursuing your specific goals for the event, you also want to get to know people and stimulate interesting conversation.

- Ahead of time, set goals for who you want to meet and what you want to accomplish.
- Plan a reward for completing your goals.
- When you talk to someone, ask questions about his or her career and listen intently. People love to talk about themselves, and most have few chances to do so.
- Be friendly, but limit your own stories and opinions to keep the focus on the other person.
- Stay professional: talk about your field, positive aspects of the event, and business topics.
- Avoid the conversation minefields of politics and religion since they likely have nothing to do with work.
- Ahead of time, select three or four current, positive topics you can bring up to bridge awkward silences.

Enter a Conversation

What if you are there alone and need to make a connection with someone who is already talking in a group? Here are some tips:

1. Approach the group, smile and listen politely for a minute or two, then say, "Please excuse me for interrupting."

2. When you are acknowledged with a look or a word, ask for what you want by saying, "I'm Susan Jones and I've heard so much about your important work, Mr. Smith. Would it be possible to meet with you another time to learn more?"

3. If you get a business card and an invitation to call for a meeting, great. If you can join the conversation, even better. But if not, smile, apologize for interrupting, and leave.

WORK TOWARD A BIAS-FREE WORKPLACE

We gain harmony and understanding when we have exposure to differences over time. When diverse people come together to solve a problem, the outcome is reduced bias and fewer feelings of discomfort. Let's unite to work together on the problem of creating equality for women. Learning to understand each other better makes that a win-win-win.

Root Out Your Own Biases

Conscious or unconscious biases make us uncomfortable with people we do not already know. The truth is, everyone has biases. It's part of being human, as we discussed in Chapter 2, and the fix is to examine our own behavior and connect on a human level. Trudy Bourgeois describes a woman who asked anxiously what she should call a woman of color. The answer, of course, was "Call her by her name!" And when you need to use a pronoun, be aware that many gender nonconforming people today might prefer pronouns that don't match your perception of their appearance. It may not be important to you, but it is important to them, so do a web search for "preferred gender pronouns" to learn more. You can also ask if your company offers diversity workshops or training, and campaign for your city, community center, church, or library to offer some. You can read online about which terms are acceptable or offensive. "*The Associated Press Stylebook* is updated every year and is a trusted reference for journalists everywhere," explained Kristal Zook. "In it, terms in common usage are listed, defined, and explained."

Bias is most difficult to see and counteract when it is our own. The gold-standard self-test for implicit bias is Harvard's Implicit Association Test (IAT). Take the test yourself at https://implicit .harvard.edu/implicit/takeatest.html and encourage others at work to do the same. Organize a time to discuss what you learned and what surprised you. Listen to yourself and others. When you receive feedback or input that brings up resistance, that's often a sign that you have some work to do in that area. Are you equally respectful and courteous toward others? Also, check your own attitudes toward the men in your workplace. They did not cause the current system in which men hold most of the power, and you can't fix it by being angry at them. Instead, identify men who support equality for women and work with them to create positive change.

Develop a New Habit to Eliminate Your Own Bias

Prejudice is a learned habit and, as such, can be unlearned, said Sarah Acer, the founder of Align Communications and Creative. She told me about the work of Patricia G. Devine, a psychology professor and prejudice researcher at the University of Wisconsin Prejudice and Intergroup Relations Lab. Devine says that changing a mental habit is not something that happens in a moment but is a focused, longer-term process, during which you practice new responses and tell new stories. Here are the steps:

- Decide on the habit you want to change.
- Notice what that habit is doing for you now.
- Believe that you can develop better attitudes.
- Choose a belief to replace the biased one.
- Stop hanging out with people who share biased beliefs.
- Visualize how good you will feel without the bias.
- Forgive yourself for not being able to change overnight and for sometimes backsliding.

Reprogram Your Brain

When women think we are not good at something, our doubts tend to make us perform more poorly at it. This is called stereotype threat. Luckily, the opposite is also true: if we believe we will do something well, our chances of doing so will increase. Who knew that focusing on our values could help our performance? Ed Yong reported in his *Discover* magazine blog, *Not Exactly Rocket Science*, which is now on *National Geographic*, that a University of Colorado physics class used a simple writing exercise to eliminate a dramatic gender gap. Asking students to write for just fifteen minutes changed their lives. Women college students no longer scored lower on physics tests than the men did, and using the same test, African American and Latino seventh and eighth graders no longer scored lower than white students on their end-of-year report cards.

A sample of the exercise, which Yong made available online, reveals that the students picked two or three items from a list, then wrote about their feelings and why these were important to them: athletic ability, being good at art, being smart or getting good grades, creativity, independence, living in the moment, membership in a social group (such as your community, racial group, or school club), music, politics, relationships with friends or family, religious values, and sense of humor.

It's possible that this internal focus and affirmation of values worked to increase confidence and reduce anxiety. It couldn't hurt, so try it for yourself by writing briefly about:

- Two or three of your values
- What is important to you and why
- The values and strengths you bring to work

Help Your Company Culture Move Away from Bias

Here are some actions you can take and things you can say, using a neutral tone, to counteract bias on a daily basis:

- Notice demeaning language, eye-rolls, and attitudes and call them out: "I noticed you rolled your eyes, which made me feel that you don't respect my comment. Is that your intention?"
- Speak out when you see or hear sexist/ageist remarks or behavior: "I have not observed that to be the case. She contributes a lot to our group and we are lucky to have her."
- Speak up for women when they are not in the room: "Susan is a very effective leader, and her team tells me she is very easy to work with."
- Exert peer pressure to treat women better: "We all have a stake in making women feel valued in our company. How can we work together to improve that?"
- Defend others when you hear a biased slur: "That's a racial slur that has nothing to do with her qualifications or performance."
- Never laugh or respond positively when others are ridiculed for whatever reason: "That's not funny. Don't make fun of her."

Manage Your Anger Intentionally

When your emotions overflow, it's best to vent in a safe place, preferably non-work-related. Glynda Carr of Higher Heights counseled that in the moment, a woman needs to step back, refocus on her goals, and use her voice and emotions to achieve those goals. For example, saying something like, "I'm angry right now. Let's talk this through tomorrow," postpones any confrontation so you can regain your composure. But on a macro level we need to reshape the narrative around women as leaders, she said. Cultural stereotypes mean an aggressive woman of color will be seen as an "angry black woman." Let's work together to redefine women leaders and reshape those narratives.

Keeping It Together

Emotional triggers can feel like legitimate threats and may overwhelm you at times. If criticism or a tense meeting makes you feel like crying, try one of these proven methods to stop tears until that choked feeling passes:

- Work on a mathematical calculation in your mind or count backward from one hundred.
- Pinch the fleshy area between your thumb and first finger. Tears come from the emotional side of your brain. Engaging the rational side will suppress your urge to cry, and the painful pinch will shift your focus.
- Hold your head up. Tears collect in the bottom eyelid. They won't run down with your head elevated.
- Before going into a challenging situation, slip a rubber band around your wrist. If you feel teary, snap it a couple of times and you'll quickly forget about crying.

WHAT TO SAY WHEN YOU HEAR HURTFUL COMMENTS

Everyone can elevate other women at work, wrote Anne Krook, chair of the board of directors of Lambda Legal, who has decades of experience as a woman in tech industries. Her special interest is integrating younger women into the workplace, preparing them for success, and coaching them to interact with colleagues. Her outstanding book on this topic, filled with specific examples, is *Now What Do I Say? Practical Workplace Advice for Younger Women.*

Here are some of her general principles for handling hurtful or critical comments at work:

- Maintain a neutral tone, especially to keep from being criticized as too emotional: "Wow. Huh. Really?"
- When defending other women, stick to a fact-based response: "She made excellent points about the Smith case that will help us clinch the deal. We are lucky to have her."
- Changing behavior and attitudes takes time (and may be impossible if the other person harbors ill will), so expect to repeat consistent messaging over time.
- If someone is telling tales to you or about you, try something like: "I'm sorry to hear that. I'll take that up with (name)."

- Repeat an all-purpose response to offensive remarks until the person stops or apologizes: "Excuse me?"
- If someone is calling you "girl" when the guys are called "men," say this: "Don't call me 'girl.' Don't use that term for me."

Follow these scripts when you hear biased remarks…

…About Race, Sexual Orientation, or Ethnicity

When you hear someone tell a woman of color, "You're so articulate!" in a surprised tone, that's a microaggression based on centuries of unfounded stereotypes.

- "Why are you surprised by her speaking skills? She's a well-educated and experienced professional."

…That Make Assumptions about Sexual Orientation

When an invitation to a work event says, "Bring your husband," an LGBTQ+ woman with a woman partner will wonder if her partner is welcome. Use gender-neutral language to reinforce inclusion.

- "Families are welcome. Bring your partner or spouse."

…That Are Rude and Intrusive

LGBTQ+ people are sometimes asked questions about sexual roles, genitals, and other inappropriate topics. When you witness or experience such questions, answer directly and set clear boundaries.

- "That is a rude and intrusive question. Don't ask her anything like that again."
- "That is too personal of a question. You are making me uncomfortable. If you'd like education on that subject, I suggest you find resources online."

...Based on Gender Stereotypes

Speak up when you hear a sexist remark. Every day snide comments or unintentional biases crop up and poison the atmosphere for women. Everyone needs to respond to these—women too.

- "I don't think Dorothy is pushy. I think she's persistent. It took real persistence to bring in that new client."
- "Alice, I'll make the coffee while you explain your project. Who needs sugar and cream?"
- "We always ask Jennie to take the lunch order for staff meetings. Let's all take turns instead. Who wants to start this week?"
- "Mark, your comments about Edie's attractiveness are embarrassing her. Let's keep our comments professional and focus on work performance instead of appearance."

...About "Women's Work"

Susan finally got tired of handling the office catering. She approached Fred, her boss, and raised the issue non-defensively: "Fred, you know I'm happy to help, but there are ten of us on the team and I've ordered the food for the past three meetings. Let's take turns sharing that responsibility."

...About Parenting Issues

Genesha wants to have a baby, but her coworkers frequently say that employees with kids aren't doing their share. She hates to be criticized and plans to take a lower-level job, just so she can be a mom in peace. But this will lower her earnings and stall her career, which she doesn't want either. What if she could defuse the snarky remarks? It's not easy, but here are some things Genesha could say:

- "I appreciate the flexibility that would let me care for my family, but I also want to do my fair share. In what way do you think I would be putting a burden on others?"

- "I understand your concern about dividing the work fairly. Did you know I come in four hours every other Saturday to make sure I do my share?"
- "As fellow parents, would you be willing to help me develop a job-sharing proposal for our boss that might better serve everyone?"
- "Boss, this company could really benefit from a work-from-home option. May I work with my coworkers to study successful examples and propose a plan?"

...About People's Appearance

Marina's predominantly male coworkers often comment on some aspect of her appearance. She can model the way she wants to be treated by responding in a professional, non-emotional way: "I would appreciate you commenting on my work performance rather than my appearance." This same advice works if you hear someone commenting on another person's appearance.

...About Age Differences

Lisa is a manager who prides herself on being intentional, equal, and kind. It takes energy and awareness to be consistent, she says, but she always tries to suggest a goal for improvement. She manages several people who are older than she is, an increasingly common situation according to the Center for Generational Kinetics. She always keeps her focus on performance rather than personality. When an older coworker makes a snide comment about her youth or treats her like a parent would, she refuses to stew over it and keeps her behavior professional: "I know it's difficult to accept leadership from someone as young as your daughter, but you can help me by honestly sharing your concerns and ideas about your job and our company goals." She leads by example. She listens carefully, a skill she has cultivated. She values and respects others. Please note that all of these have been regarded as stereotypically "feminine" behaviors.

...About Age Difference and Gender

Lisa also supervises several young men who exhibit low self-confidence and poor decision making. She always tries to point out the good things by saying, "I want to see more of that." Every employee appreciates courtesy, mentoring, coaching, guidance, encouragement, trust, and safety rather than criticism, fear, intimidation, and punishment.

WORK FOR EQUAL PAY

Unequal pay is a serious form of bias against women. To find out if pay scales are equivalent:

- **Ask people in your company what they earn.** Although some employers discourage workers from discussing wages, the National Labor Relations Act made that illegal in 1935. There are exceptions, of course, so do your research. California's Fair Pay Act, which strengthened the preexisting Equal Pay Act and was signed into law in 2015, explicitly stated "that retaliation against employees who seek to enforce the law is illegal" and made "it illegal for employers to prohibit employees from discussing or inquiring about their co-workers' wages."
- **Ask people in your network what they earn.** California's Equal Pay Act also "eliminates the requirement that the jobs that are compared must be located at the same establishment," but remember to take into account differences in an area's cost of living.
- **Find out if your state is one of the ten that forbid employers from basing a salary on previous earnings.** This practice has long kept women earning less.
- **Go online.** Visit websites like www.glassdoor.com and www.thebalancecareers.com/salaries-for-jobs-a-z-list-2063402 for national information on pay scales. Or check out an app called Blind, which allows users to carry on anonymous conversations in their company or industry. Discussions of compensation and critiques of job offers are popular topics that receive lots of comments.

Prepare a Business Case

Once you have gathered actual numbers, work together with others to develop the business case for gender equity. Does the company struggle to maintain its staff? How will pay equity improve the company's ability to attract and retain good workers? Estimate how equity will improve company morale and productivity. If you can, report the results in profit-and-loss terms that a bottom line–oriented boss would understand. Would establishing equal pay bring good publicity to the company? Would maintaining unequal pay threaten the company's federal or other contracts? Progressive company managers will be open to the idea, so do a web search for "company pay audit" to review the many available tools.

Strategize Your Presentation

Practice your pitch together, then pick someone to approach a company leader you consider to be a trusted advisor and start a friendly and positive conversation. Mention how important equal pay is to you and that you want your company to benefit from doing the right thing and showing employees that their concerns are being heard. Make clear that you are not threatening but rather wanting to help the company succeed, and that actions toward equity will actually protect them from legal problems.

CHART YOUR COURSE

If you've tried every move to change your company culture and little or no change has occurred, there are a multitude of options: seek a lateral transfer, look for another job, start your own company, go back to school, retool your career. Following are some things to consider before you give notice.

Identify What You Want

Can you answer the question, "What do you want?" Marlene Chism advised in a newsletter that if you can't, "it may be because you have already decided that what you want would be way too difficult, take too much time, and would prevent you from doing other things." Are you coming from a place of scarcity rather than abundance? Notice if you are telling yourself things like:

- *It would take too long.*
- *I already know what he would say.*
- *I've tried it before and it didn't work.*
- *There's not much time.*
- *I'm too old.*

These statements show that you might be feeling overwhelmed by and stuck in your current situation, whether in work or in life. Imagine removing the barriers you think are in your way. Now see how easily you can speak about what you want. If it were easy, and if you had enough time, what would you want?

Clarify Your Goals

Smart women take responsibility for their lives and experiences. You are more likely to get what you want if you know what that is, create a clear road map to get there, and ask for it. Ask other women you trust to help you:

- Think deeply about your goals: "I always wanted to…" "One of my highest values is…" "My friend, what do you see as my greatest strengths?"
- Set your intentions and make a plan: "This is what I want, so what steps could I take to make it happen?"
- Seek out mentors you can ask for advice: "I admire you and would like to learn from your experiences. Would you be willing to meet me Tuesday for coffee and talk?"
- Read leadership books and listen to relevant podcasts: "Let's both read this book and talk about the interesting nuggets we pick up."

- Ask for help: "Family/friend, are you willing to support and advise me while I figure this out? How are you willing to help me?"

Define Yourself

At Take The Lead's international rollout in 2014 motivational speaker and finance expert Carla Harris delivered the keynote address, which is available on *YouTube*. Harris described the importance of intentionally training people to think about you in the way you want by using consistent language and behavior. She said this is crucial for women because all the important decisions about your career—compensation, promotion, and new assignments—will be made when you are not in the room. What characteristics will help you advance? Harris said:

- Name the top three adjectives that describe your company's values (they will be on the website).
- Name the top three adjectives that define who you truly are.
- Where those words intersect are the traits that will bring success in your job. Look for ways to repeatedly work those words into your language and behavior for ninety days.

Harris recalled that early in her career a senior manager questioned whether she was tough enough for her male-dominated Wall Street company. She was chagrined to be ambushed by this gendered stereotype but decided that for ninety days she would walk tough, talk tough, eat tough, drink tough, and use the word *tough* in her language when talking about herself. With consistent behavior and language, Harris changed management's perception and positioned herself for advancement. If you think it and walk it, you can become it. Practice being who you want to be. Try it out on family and friends. While you're at it, recruit your allies at work to also use these words to describe you, and make sure you return the favor.

Strategize to Advance the Way You Want To

You have a line job in which you are responsible for a modest profit-and-loss statement. Your boss admires your communication skills and offers you a promotion to a staff position in human resources. You would get a raise, but will it really help further your goals? Staff roles rarely lead to C-suite positions because responsibility for bringing in money enhances status and power. Consider saying this instead:

I appreciate that you recognize my communication skills. But I'd like to move into a higher line position where I can continue to grow company profits. What would I need to do to qualify? Will you help me?

Consider Becoming Your Own Boss

Say your current job has a lousy work-life balance. Would starting your own business improve that? Millions of women consider it their best option. Here are some benefits:

- You will be able to make your own rules and choices.
- Your work will be your passion and your passion will be your work.

There are also these cons to weigh:

- You will incur all the financial risks without a sure paycheck.
- Time demands may at times be even worse, although you will set the schedule.

If it feels overwhelming to start your own business, see if there's anything you can do to change your current situation:

- Could you introduce some self-determination at your current job?
- Would changing policy and culture make you happier there?

- By joining forces with others, what could you change to make work better for everyone?

SUCCESSFUL WOMEN ADVANCE AND EARN MORE

If we want to increase our earning power, we have to be willing to look deeply within ourselves and then do the work. Learning is a life-long process, and if you have stopped learning at your job, it's time to move on. The following suggestions reflect the combined professional experience of scores of members of the Ozarks Alliance of Professional Organizations.

Improve your job performance:
- Perform at your highest level.
- Get employer expectations in writing.
- Ask for feedback between performance evaluations.
- Document your performance.
- Ask for evaluations and disciplinary actions in writing.
- Take criticism seriously, not personally.
- Work to correct problems.

Increase your pay:
- Ask for specifics on pay ranges.
- Ask how you can be more valuable to your organization.
- Ask for specifics on what to do to earn pay increases.
- Ask about matching programs for retirement savings.

Increase your value:
- Be willing to learn new skills.
- Take on new assignments.
- Do the extra 10 percent.
- Take advantage of tuition reimbursement programs.
- Never gossip, complain, or exert negative influence.
- Make promptness a habit and don't take too much sick time.

Develop yourself personally:

- Don't ally yourself too closely with one supervisor or mentor.
- Know what you want.
- Set priorities for what's most important in your life and career.
- Be flexible.
- Prepare to be lucky, and don't be surprised when you get the advancement that you deserve.

Communicate Your Promote-ability

Every company has standards of communication, which may be compiled in an employee handbook but are often unwritten. Isabella Clivilez-Wu laid out general rules for business emails in a *Forbes* article and urged following basic professional guidelines. Write the way you would like to be spoken to by your boss (not by your BFF), calmly and with courtesy (avoid ALL CAPS, high priority, and reply all). Avoid abbreviations and slang. Read through before hitting send, and add courtesy: *hello, please, thank you, sincerely.*

Of course, you will also figure out the company dress code by watching the way others dress. Notice the ones who are doing the job you want and dress the way they do. Unless you're in tech or a creative field, it's typically better to dress in simple, conservative clothes. You want people to remember how helpful and skilled you are, rather than the slogan on your T-shirt, the tattoo on your shoulder, or the color of your bra. Better they should forget what you wore and remember your friendly and useful professional self.

Figure Out How to Help

Have you ever asked someone to help when you were overwhelmed and had that person stand in the middle of a chaotic room and say, "Okay, tell me what to do"? Sometimes that just adds to your stress. You would rather team up with a person who can scan a room, spot something that needs doing, and do it without being told. Be that person. Successful women apply this at work too. They observe, see what needs to be done next to achieve company goals, and do it.

As you develop your strategy for what to say and do to help yourself and other women advance, remember that no one gets what they want without asking for it. Historically, courageous women have asked for outlandish things, and finally, after years of hard work and persistence, they got it. Set your sights high because you never know when that decisive person will say yes, or your timing will be exactly right to achieve something you may have thought impossible. Nothing is impossible for women when we support one another and exercise our power to work together.

Part 2

UNWINDING YOUR TWISTED SISTERS

In a perfect world everyone would be kind and thoughtful to each other, but you can encounter a bully in any walk of life. Nearly a third of workplace bullies are women who—like all bullies—most often pick on women. Women first encounter relational aggression as girls in the schoolyard and can still encounter it as adults. Understanding why women behave this way can make it easier to cope with and navigate the barriers and biases commonly found at work and in life.

By thinking it through, women can overcome their anxieties and stand up to these bullies, reducing their power. The ideal solution is not to expose the bully to shame and humiliation but to turn the bully into an ally, or at least to neutralize his or her disruptive behavior. By increasing communication and releasing your own internalized sexist attitudes, you can help grow a supportive community and end infighting.

We describe specific work scenarios and offer strategies from experts for de-escalating woman-on-woman bullying. Whether the strategy is winning over a bully or going around her, we provide scripts you can tailor for yourself and practice to defeat bullying and make your company a place you cannot *wait* to go!

CHAPTER 5
WHAT MAKES WOMEN MEAN?

"I learned compassion from being discriminated against. Everything bad that's ever happened to me has taught me compassion.**"**

ELLEN DEGENERES, comedian

So many women have asked me, "Why are women so mean to other women?" Of all the challenges they face at work, this seems to cause women the most angst. Perhaps women take greater offense at bullying by their female coworkers because they have been trained to expect bullying behavior from men. Perhaps they have bought into the stereotype (against all evidence from the schoolyard and beyond) that women are sugar and spice and will automatically be nurturing and supportive of other women.

Whatever the cause of their pain and frustration, the short answer to the question is that women are mean for the same reasons men are mean. They are not demons to be feared or destroyed, just unhappy people. I want to explain the psychological basis of these toxic behaviors to help you identify and understand what's going on, so you can respond with compassion. It's hardly ever personal, so don't let it derail you at work.

Studies show that 60–70 percent of bullies at work are men; 30–40 percent are women, and they all target women two-thirds of the time, according to a 2017 survey conducted by the Workplace Bullying Institute (WBI). The term *bully* has been associated with men's physical violence and aggression, so sociologists have coined another term, *relational aggression*, to describe the more covert emotional and psychological aggressions used to damage a victim's social status and relationships, which are often practiced by women and girls. The overlap in techniques and emotional costs, however, makes bullying and relational aggression virtually indistinguishable.

The Workplace Bullying Institute defines bullying at work as a person or group being singled out by another person for unreasonable, embarrassing, or intimidating mistreatment that harms the health of one or more persons. This is abusive conduct—threatening, humiliating, intimidating, or sabotaging—that prevents work from getting done. This definition describes relational aggression as well.

TYPES OF RELATIONAL AGGRESSION

In the workplace, emotional bullying can appear as:

- Name-calling or teasing
- Sabotage, where a woman will intentionally lie or destroy the work of others to discredit them
- Starting rumors (often false) that destroy a woman's reputation (often concerning her lifestyle or appearance)
- Taking personal belongings from refrigerator or desk
- Backstabbing (where women will gain someone's confidence and then use private and often delicate information to harm her)
- Taking undeserved credit for the work of others and even forbidding subordinates from presenting their own work to upper management
- Slut-shaming (when women suggest things like "she got her job just because she looked hot" or "she took her turn on the casting couch")

- Social alienation, in which a clique of women deliberately excludes a coworker from the group by rejecting or shunning her

Outright physical abuse is less common, since direct bullying of that nature is against the law, although it still occurs in the most toxic environments. However, the psychological and verbal abuse that women inflict at work is much more common and extremely damaging.

Workplace bullying is so common in various forms that almost three-fourths of employees have been affected by bullying, either as a target or a witness, according to research from Dr. Judith Lynn Fisher-Blando with the University of Phoenix. In fact, WBI has reported that bullying on the job is four times more common than either sexual harassment or racial discrimination.

Reality Doesn't Match Many Women's Expectations

Fortunately, in my experience, *most* women are warm and supportive, but that perspective may create unrealistic expectations about *all* women. You might expect "that women leaders will all be more nurturing than males and everything will be wonderful," said Dr. Gary Namie, who cofounded WBI. "But...women are just as capable of being tyrannical as men," he told reporter Tessa Cheek. "If the corporate structure rewards aggression, they [women] will be aggressive."

Men have developed ritualized ways to resolve competition and aggression, such as when they play sports or punch each other in the schoolyard. But since women have been taught to conceal their feelings, they often let things fester. At work the bully may be a person in a position of authority who feels threatened, or a coworker who is immature or insecure. People most frequently display unprofessional aggressive behavior when they feel somehow "less than" the other person, especially if the company has role models at the top who encourage such behavior as a way to gain power.

MOTIVES AND METHODS FOR MEANNESS

Whether it's called bullying, bitchiness, relational or indirect aggression, or something else, women who behave this way can make you dread going to work. Although the vast majority of women are not mean, the ones who *are* inflict a lot of pain and frustration. They disrupt the workplace out of proportion to their numbers because even people who are not targeted are affected by it.

Psychologists know that in their hearts bullies have low self-esteem and feel powerless, insecure, and unhappy. The reasons for meanness will vary with the person, background, and situation, but bullies are not evil. They are just ordinary people who are being mean to someone else. Their behavior typically indicates that they are unhappy because no happy person is mean to others. Deep inside they are sad, maybe even afraid, and some people express these feelings as anger.

> **If I stop to kick every barking dog, I am not going to get where I'm going.**
>
> JACKIE JOYNER-KERSEE,
> Olympic athlete

Mean People Usually Had Mean Role Models

I know from observation that unhappy girls have often learned from unhappy role models. The "mean girls" you hear about may have mean parents at home who criticize them or make them feel inadequate, abuse or neglect them, or inflict some other damage to their self-esteem that makes them strike out to hurt others. Often these influential adults are insecure, overly competitive, and have trouble accepting themselves or others. They lack self-esteem, and they may view women who exhibit confidence—including their young daughters—as challengers and seek to tear them down. These unhappy people cannot stand to be around happy people, and they frequently become abusive trying to inflict their unhappiness on others. In their sad world there is always someone who is thinner, prettier, smarter, richer, or luckier, whom they can envy and resent.

Children pick up on these parental behaviors quickly. By the age of four most girls are learning to manipulate other children. Educators tell us that by age five girls can skillfully gossip, keep secrets, and tell lies to exclude a targeted peer, often someone close to them whom they envy in some way. Around age eight nearly all girls begin to question their self-worth and form cliques that target or exclude other girls.

> Around age eight nearly all girls begin to question their self-worth and form cliques that target or exclude other girls.

Girl bullies are often popular, pretty, and admired by teachers, and many have been targets of bullies themselves. Surprisingly, these girls may not realize that they are behaving like bullies. They normalize it because Mom acts that way; they see it happening on TV and every day in politics. If no one teaches them to stop it, they develop into mean teens, using cruel methods like cyberbullying, verbal attacks, spreading gossip, and shunning. Unfortunately, we've seen cases where mothers aided and even instigated verbal or online attacks their teen girls made on a schoolmate. By the time girls grow up and get their first job, this behavior may already be ingrained.

Learned Passive Aggression

Another key form that emotional bullying can take is passive aggression. In American society girls are expected to stifle their normal feelings of anger, fear, jealousy, and hurt and behave as if they are sweet and nice, sugar and spice. This cultural expectation promotes covert aggression. Girls learn to hide their true agendas. Because they are typically punished for directly pursuing their goals, they learn to use a passive aggressive, indirect, and manipulative approach to get what they want.

The overriding goal of relational aggression, also known as emotional bullying, is to give the perpetrator a sense of control. They exercise power through humiliation of a target. At school this behavior might have been reinforced by kids taunting others, fearful teachers, or willfully blind administrators.

Cultural Factors

Our culture particularly enjoys a "catfight," so much so that it's a frequent storyline in film and entertainment. This harms women's prospects for advancement by reinforcing the idea that women are unfit for leadership and exist only to be looked at. Reality TV shows that capitalize on women being mean to other women position this as normal behavior and go so far as to make stars of women who behave badly. But don't believe everything you see and hear. Reality TV is scripted and staged, over and over again, so it's a mistake to model your behavior on what you see there. Disrespect is everywhere, too, and popular media ridicule our most popular stars and politicians for everything from bad hairdos to serious drug problems.

Who Does She Think She Is?

Consider the classic female question, "Who does she think she is?" We've all heard it at some point in our lives, whether directed at us or at someone else. It's what women bullies say when they're trying to keep a woman in her place. Women may perceive a woman supervisor as a weak leader and refuse to take direction from her, or gossip behind her back to undermine her. It also happens to ambitious women who may demonstrate skills that others do not have, or to those women who seek support to advance.

As I rose in my career and pursued my education, so-called friends (even family) said, "Who do you think you are?" when I expected my husband to care for our children. If this happens to you, my advice is don't take it personally, but remember that you are making your mark on history. I wanted to set an example for my daughters so they would not be afraid to pursue any goal they chose. I'm happy to report that all three of them got the message and I'm a proud mama of three successful women.

This was important to me because women have traditionally been trained to toe the line and serve men's agendas rather than their own. Any woman who breaks out of that to serve her own agenda can be resented and condemned for trying to rise "above herself," and for stepping outside the prevailing expectations of the office clique.

One of my podcast guests, Roxi Hewertson, used the term *reference group* to describe the enforcers who maintain such norms. This social psychology term applies to any group we want to fit into, including our working world. The reference group comprises both the people who would keep us behaving like them and ourselves once we adapt our behavior to fit in. When more than one reference group has power at work, a chaotic work environment generates drama and controversy.

Addiction to Drama

Some people crave drama the same way an addict craves a drug, and this can become an instigator for emotional bullying. The adrenaline released by conflict makes them feel alive. Precipitating a conflict makes them feel in charge. The term *drama queen* actually does pertain to a person who seems to live for drama and creates as much as possible in everyday life. Few things are more destructive to productivity in the workplace.

Performance, Not Personality

When a person or group engages in bullying at work, it creates a toxic work environment. It's obvious when there's a problem: productivity lags, absenteeism increases, employee turnover accelerates, and profitability declines. It's bad for the health and welfare of the people, and it's bad for business. This is clearly a performance problem, not a personality issue. Everyone knows who the bullies are, and in a healthy company an effective manager will stop the behavior before it hurts the company. Unfortunately, that doesn't happen nearly as often as we wish, but there are still things you can do to change your relationship with a bully.

HOW TO COMBAT RELATIONAL AGGRESSION

Wouldn't it be better to turn a mean woman into a powerful team player than to allow her to tear the team apart? The healing ingredient that stops a cycle of abuse is often a positive male or female role model who takes time to treat the bully with kindness and to offer friendly and firm guidance. This is powerful medicine that enables people to change their behavior and values. Clients have told me many times that all it took was a *single person* offering kind support to enable them to believe in themselves and create a better life.

When you encounter a mean woman at work, rather than reacting with shocked silence, anxiety, and avoidance, be that person who draws clear boundaries while modeling kindness, gratitude for her gifts, and admiration for her skills. Encourage her to develop healthy self-confidence and self-esteem. Women move forward more quickly when we treat each other with love and compassion.

Women move forward more quickly when we treat each other with love and compassion.

Our workplaces need more women and girls who display empathy and care for others. Confidence and gratitude go hand in hand with happiness, while fear and jealousy go hand in hand with meanness. Treat the people around you with confidence and gratitude and you are choosing happiness as your state of mind.

Learn from Bullying

Learning to stand up for yourself and make a bully stop is a rite of passage for many children. Women ultimately need to learn to regard bad behavior as a gift because it forces you to decide how you want to be treated, said Marlene Chism. "The good thing about experiencing unwanted emotions is you get to claim what is totally unacceptable."

> Bullies may target a high-performing woman at work who stands out rather than blending in because they fear the overachiever will make them look bad.

You might assume that the targets of workplace bullying are the weakest players, but in fact they are often the strongest, according to WBI. Rather than being the loners, weird, or simply people who don't fit in, as is often the case with schoolyard bullying, the reverse is commonly true at work. People who are more skilled, more technically proficient, and even more liked may become targets because something about them makes the bully feel threatened.

Bullies may target a high-performing woman at work who stands out rather than blending in because they fear the overachiever will make them look bad, said diversity advocate Dr. Sheila Robinson. This can happen in manufacturing, where line workers systematically pressure the fastest worker to slow down to prevent their quotas from being raised, and in white-collar settings, where a woman who impresses the boss with special expertise can be deeply resented and ultimately driven out.

Bullying behaviors can also be motivated by biases against people of color, diverse faiths, and gender nonconforming identities. Sometimes these forms of bullying start out with subtle microaggressions or what appear to be in-group/out-group dynamics, and they communicate the bully's dominance and rejection of another person's identity.

ENABLERS ENFORCE "POWER OVER"

Women who have gained power at work within a male-dominated, sexist system often enforce that system to protect their hard-won status. In effect, they perpetuate the traditional old models because they cannot imagine succeeding any other way. They have no faith that they can change the system, so they do their best to survive within it. When people feel powerless to influence the structure, they tend to "kick the dog" to manage their frustration. In many cases the "dog" is another woman since she is often the least powerful member in the system.

In a company with a traditional structure masculinity and power are bound together, just like femininity and service. This isn't an attack on men; it's just that almost everyone holds these ideas about gender—including you and me—and they lurk far below the level of consciousness.

Queen Bee Syndrome

Women managers sometimes seek to protect their status in a hierarchy dominated by men by being overly tough on their female employees, solely because they are women. This "Queen Bee Syndrome" is a real phenomenon, according to University of Arizona management professor Allison Gabriel, who conducted a large study. She found that women who display traditionally masculine traits, such as dominance, are especially targeted. Women of color may be targeted more if cultural differences cause their behavior to be perceived as masculine and therefore uncomfortable for other women. Behaviors like ignoring, interrupting, mocking, and other disrespectful treatment are used to put them back in their place and keep them from threatening the Queen Bee.

"We primates live in social groups because there is safety in numbers and it's easy to find mates," wrote Meredith Small in reference to the work of Adrienne Nishina of the University of California at Davis. "But group living is not always easy; every individual is self-serving and yet everyone has to get along." In particularly competitive human environments, like Hollywood and hard-driving corporations, women employ psychological warfare to align themselves with a powerful man at the top of the ladder.

WHEN WOMEN OPPRESS WOMEN

When bullies cannot fault another woman for her performance, they often resort to slut-shaming. The suggestion that she got her job just because she looked "hot," or that she took her turn on the casting couch, is demeaning and devastating to women working hard to advance. Targets are often confident in many areas, including their looks, and a bully who feels threatened may seek to reestablish her control or influence. She may launch a campaign of disrespect, gossip, and public humiliation in hopes of driving out her competition. "The tendency of women to perpetuate rigid gender roles and to oppress other women is referred to as internalized misogyny," wrote Kaz Weida in an article for *Rantt Media*. We called this *internalized sexism* in Chapter 2.

Women usually don't see their own ingrained prejudice when they "open conversations with little girls by complimenting cute clothes or carefully styled hair. It's the way we admonish women to be considerate, to subjugate their own needs for those of others," Weida explained. "After centuries of conditioning when it comes to gender roles, it's not something we should be blamed for....But we do need to acknowledge that women can [be] and are sometimes the agents of their own oppression. And be aware of our own bias so we can work to overcome it and not let it perpetuate itself in our personal and political choices."

A classic example is activist and author Phyllis Schlafly, who famously led the charge to defeat the Equal Rights Amendment in the early 1970s. She believed women should marry, have children, and rely on men to provide and protect. As a personal decision this is fine, and every couple arrives at their own terms. Many women appreciate a man who leads the way. However, setting this as the standard for *all* leaves out the millions of women who are the sole support or primary earners in their families, or who want to explore different possibilities for their lives.

Those who insist that women stay in their traditional "feminine" roles unknowingly hold all women back. It's an insidious way that our culture works to perpetuate the status quo. Women get praised for being model women—model wives and mothers who are pretty, nicely dressed, and behaving sweetly. Why wouldn't they perpetuate the system that earns them praise and elevates them in a culture of rewards and punishments?

Enforcement by women is painfully effective because we fear they will judge and exclude us from female society. You've observed this, I'm sure. When a woman does excel and achieve a higher position, some women will examine her in ways that have nothing to do with her education or job experience. They will ridicule her clothes, hair, makeup, style, walk—anything to demean her or damn her with a backhanded compliment. After I received my doctorate in clinical psychology and passed my licensing exam, more than one person said to me, "Wow, I didn't think you were that smart." They watched me complete four years of college, earn a master's degree, and endure two years of post-grad education, and all that time they thought I was not intelligent? Ouch!

Some women act like they are supporting other women when really "they want the attention of the corporate male because they still feel that the men have the power," wrote international philanthropist Linda Rendleman on her website. Women may be reluctant to raise other women to their own level. Instead, "they become jealous. They become closed. They want to be 'Queen of the Hill' and another woman is threatening to them. They fear losing their place."

"Men notice what women say about each other," Rendleman continued. But "when women support one another we are strong. If we talk behind another woman's back to a man we are perpetuating stereotypes that women are weak. When we harm one woman we are ultimately harming ourselves."

MUTUAL SUPPORT COMBATS BULLYING

Women can really help each other deal with bullying behavior through mutual support because bullies are less likely to target someone who has willing helpers around. It's also true that commiseration and support can help keep the situation in perspective. Joining or starting a group of like-minded colleagues can help you get through difficult times.

Even though I was grown, married, and a mom, I struggled with criticism from other women when I decided to pursue my doctorate. Several women undermined my nontraditional choice by asking, "Who is going to take care of your family?" I hated feeling that lack of support and decided to build a community of like-minded women who would support each other, women who realized that when we help one another, anything is possible. I found that community with the women I call my Psyche Sisters. All eight of us were seasoned therapists working on our doctorates in clinical psychology. We gave each other moral, physical, and emotional support, and all eight of us received our doctorates and became licensed psychologists. We have continued for more than twenty years to meet, reflect, encourage, and celebrate who we are as women and psychologists.

Check Your Bias

Before going to war, take a searching and honest look at yourself and the situation you're facing:

- Is there any way you might be misinterpreting what's going on?
- Are you the victim of a bullying campaign, or just upset by someone's manner or tone?
- Does this person treat everyone that way or just you?
- Are you treating everyone with the same courtesy and respect, or are you being high-handed and demanding to some?
- Are you performing your job as well as you can, or are you making life difficult for others?
- Might a coworker have cause to be annoyed with you?

If this isn't a bullying situation, what can you learn from it? How can you adjust your behavior? The Australian blog *Now To Love* referenced the work of Meredith Fuller, author of *Working with Mean Girls*, with regard to this topic. From her research, Fuller developed several categories of "mean girls," including "Nota-Bitch: She disagrees with you, reminds you to complete tasks you are required to do, reinforces office protocols and holds you accountable." While our culture has pitted us against other women and trained us to label such assertive women as "mean girls," we might actually learn a lot from a strong woman like that.

In our society today women work outside the home in numbers roughly equal to men. But the power players are still overwhelmingly men, and masculine leadership styles dominate most corporate cultures. Many women who have risen within this structure adopt these leadership styles to gain approval and advance. As a carryover from the days when companies would hire a single token woman to avoid charges of gender discrimination, some women imagine there's no more room at their level. This keeps women jockeying for a limited number of positions and stepping on the hands of others who try to climb the ladder.

"Women have been trained as caretakers and servants and often feel obligated to advance men's agendas rather than their own," said Dr. Sheila Robinson in our podcast interview. Unfortunately, other women suffer from this behavior.

If the Bully Is Your Boss

It's essential to strategize to achieve the results we want, and we also need to look realistically at the forces (possibly including our bosses) working against our success. A dysfunctional, old-model power structure often fosters bullying and allows employees to keep fighting among themselves, damages productivity, and keeps people too distracted and demoralized to improve the situation. If you are willing to fight to change the culture, you may find that others will join you.

However, as the late Peter Drucker reportedly said, "Culture eats strategy for breakfast." Look critically at the company culture to expose its blend of psychology, attitudes, actions, and beliefs. This will help you decide if you have a long-term future there. A strong, inclusive culture flourishes with a clear set of values and norms, insightful and equitable leaders, and employees who are confident and empowered. A weak, divisive culture, on the other hand, features dissention in the ranks, bullying and infighting, and disengaged employees who aspire only to collect their next paycheck. If the bully is highly placed and has been there a long time, it's unlikely that one person will be able to change this, so it's probably wise to polish up your résumé and move on.

COPING WITH CLIQUES

The norm for social cliques at work is actually the "boys' club," often featuring drinks, sports, and activities from which women are excluded. But when women say their office is dominated by cliques, they're probably talking about groups of women who have much less power. This may be a tight-knit group of coworkers who innocently go to lunch or meet for happy hour, or they may engage in exclusion, bullying, gossip, criticism, and other negative behaviors that cause high school–style misery.

"At work, joining a clique can give you a feeling of security, a sense of identity," said Katherine Crowley, coauthor of *Mean Girls at Work* and *Working with You Is Killing Me*, reported by Jacquelyn Smith in a *Forbes* article. "We find that office cliques tend to form most in corporate environments with weak management. They are like office gangs that emerge to fill in the void of leadership."

Cliques, like individual bullying behavior, offer a way to find safety, power, and belonging, especially through the exclusion of others. Be aware, though, that cliques and divisions at work can hamper your individual advancement. Even if you do your job well, coworkers may look critically at you because of the company you keep.

MAKE BUSINESS CASE TO CORRECT BULLYING

In her *Psychology Today* blog post "9 Tips to Manage Adult Bullying," psychologist Ellen Hendriksen wrote about the importance of correcting the bullying behavior immediately to prevent it from becoming entrenched. If your efforts to stop it don't work and you need to report it to a supervisor, relate the facts without whining. "Most importantly, be ready to talk about the problem in terms of the bottom line. Emphasize that your bully's behavior is costing the business in terms of money, time, performance, and morale." If coworkers have been driven away, tally the turnover costs, headhunter fees, lost productivity, and training and startup expenses. "Talk about productivity and how stress, distraction, and discord caused by the bully end up costing the whole team and the business at large. If possible, calculate everything out in dollars."

A May 2018 US Supreme Court decision upheld a company's right to include arbitration clauses in employment contracts. This is bad news for combatting bullying or harassment, both situations in which mediation has been proven ineffective. "Mediation is great for resolving conflict where both sides want the conflict to be resolved," Hendriksen wrote. "But that's not the case with bullying. The bully has nothing to gain from mediation."

Chapter 6 discusses ways you can work to extinguish bullying, and Chapter 7 provides specific scripts you can use. Learning to deal with conflict in positive ways, practicing good communication skills with everyone at work, and exhibiting understanding and compassion will help transform the company into a productive, positive place where you and your coworkers can build your careers together.

SUPPORT THE WOMAN, BAN THE BULLY

" Be kind, for everyone you meet is fighting a hard battle. **"**

IAN MACLAREN, Scottish author and theologian

We go to work to do our jobs and advance in our business or organization, but a workplace bully can derail a day or even a whole career. Using the ideas in this chapter could help ensure that this doesn't happen to you. Who knows, you might even get to be the hero if you can bring a bully around to becoming more of a team player and a more productive member of the work group.

STOP MEANNESS AT WORK

To stop mean women and their bullying, look for ways to support the person but extinguish the annoying behaviors. I believe the best way to end everything from catfights to downright abusive behaviors at work is with a loving, supportive community of women. As mentioned in Chapter 5, some women are so addicted to drama or chaos that they constantly create it. Experts working in recovery tell us that the opposite of addiction is community, which means our connections with others can heal us and offer the best chance of eliminating drama. At work your focus needs to be on maintaining your work performance, so it's best not to allow your emotions to overwhelm your adult common sense.

To keep your focus think deeply and reconnect with your professional ideals. What did you hope to accomplish when you came to this job? Did you want to learn new skills, demonstrate competence, and advance your career? Focus on those goals, because reacting to a mean coworker will only sidetrack you. You do not have to react to her actions.

You can avoid escalating the drama if you don't join the crowd or retaliate. Staying on the high road saves you energy and makes you a better role model for your work group. "There is a need for professionalism, which means not leaving people out, talking behind their backs, or calling them out publicly for things that aren't directly related to work," wrote Emily Blake in *Filler*. That also means not making the "offhand remark about how many calories are in their sandwich or how you didn't realize they were still making chinos with pleats. When it comes to the personal, remind yourself [that] it is none of your business if it's not about business."

One classic manipulative strategy is, *Let's you and her fight*, in which a manipulator instigates conflict between two other people. Falling for this tactic robs us of energy for building productive relationships. If we get sidetracked into attacking another woman, we're much less likely to organize and fight for equality for all.

> If we get sidetracked into attacking another woman, we're much less likely to organize and fight for equality for all.

Women are great at making connections when we put aside judgment and criticisms, like *what she wore, what she said, what did she mean, who does she think she is?* All of those topics increase separation and division. It's much more productive to focus on what we share in common—our experiences, hopes, and dreams—and how we can help each other. We certainly don't need to agree with everything someone says or does, but it is good to give her the benefit of the doubt.

Accept That Some People Won't Like You

When working to strengthen community, it's best to notice and set aside unrealistic expectations about the workplace. Good managers know that not everyone is going to like them, and they must get used to feeling uncomfortable. It is also unrealistic to expect to like and enjoy working with everyone in your department. The truth is, you do not have to like someone to work effectively with her. Your coworker doesn't have to like you either. As long as you can agree on business goals, you can create a positive relationship at work. When building your alliances strategically and consciously, it makes sense to choose the people who avoid creating drama and approach work with a cooperative and goal-oriented business focus.

Be Patient As You Build Trust

Whether in life or at work, you may expect other women to automatically support you from Day One, but in reality developing a trusting, supportive relationship takes time. Beware of the instant best friend. If you take your time opening up and expect others to do the same, you will be less likely to find yourself in an uncomfortable relationship with someone who is excessively needy or manipulative.

Avoid Intimate Friendships at Work

It also helps to shed the attitude that you have a right to know everything about your coworkers' personal lives. It's often better *not* to try for intimate relationships on the job to avoid personalizing your differences. It's just work. Also consider this: if you rise up the management ladder, having intimate friendships with people you may one day supervise can make it difficult to correct poor job performance. It's easier to stay a little detached from work if you don't let it become your world. Instead, continue to invest in your personal life. It will be easier to shrug off frustrations and disappointments at work if you cultivate a strong support system and close friends outside the workplace.

Stay Calm

In the previous chapter I talked about how bullies are not the personification of evil but just ordinary people who are being mean to others, most likely because they're unhappy themselves. Remember that being bullied isn't your fault, and remain calm as you work on the problem.

To prevent the bully from wreaking havoc in your workplace, you have to confront these behaviors in a courteous, professional, and consistent manner. That's easy to say and hard to do, but you *can* do it. You might be worried that she will retaliate and punish you with shunning and ridicule, or you might dread a confrontation. Remember that you are grown-up now and can handle tough interpersonal situations. Would it be so terrible to read a book while you eat your lunch alone for a while? People are watching to see how you react, so staying calm and centered will help de-escalate the situation. Things can change quickly, and a bully may move on.

Reclaim Your Self-Confidence

Before you confront a bully, it's a good idea to bolster your self-confidence, which might have suffered if you have encountered frequent criticism. Here are three useful strategies you can implement no matter what you are facing at work:

- **Look inward** and acknowledge that you are human. You are *awesome* (of course) and yet also capable of aggression, spitefulness, cruelty, vanity, pettiness, and so many more embarrassing behaviors. Accepting this will enable you to adopt more realistic expectations about yourself and other women.

- **Pump up your stress management program** and take outstandingly good care of yourself. You need to be strong for this effort, so claim your power. You have favorite forms of stress relief, don't you? If you don't, adopt some. This is important.
- **Love yourself** and find support outside the office. It's normal to look to other women for support and approval, and it's equally normal for them not to grant it and to gossip, hold grudges, spread rumors, slander, and ostracize instead. Find support in other parts of your life so you can feel strong and secure at work.

Now you are ready to look outward at your relationship with the bully.

DEFINE BOUNDARIES TO STOP BULLYING

It's important to verify that suspected bullying is not a product of your imagination, but it's probably best not to discuss this at work. That can easily escalate the problem. "When we fail to set boundaries and hold people accountable, we feel used and mistreated," pointed out Brené Brown in her book *The Gifts of Imperfection*. Setting boundaries is a vital way of taking care of yourself. It doesn't make you mean, selfish, or uncaring; you are a woman in control of her life deciding what treatment she will and will not allow.

> **"I'm deeply aware that whatever I give out comes back to me multiplied. This is true everywhere, including at work."**
>
> LOUISE HAY, author

In order to set boundaries you need to understand where your personal limits are. You can learn this by paying close attention to the way you feel, noticing what you can tolerate and what makes you uncomfortable and stressed. These feelings clarify your limits. This really is all about you, so instead of comparing your limits with others', focus on what works best for you. This is your choice, not theirs.

IMPROVE COMMUNICATION AT WORK

Good communication, both personal and organizational, helps employees feel connected, which in turn increases productivity. This book offers lots of ideas about improving interpersonal communication in support of other women. You may also be able to work with other women to improve company communication within the workplace. Internal communication is the glue that holds an organization together, and patient attention and clearly defined channels help employees know what is going on and how they fit. If management approves, you may be able to form a committee to recommend improvements in internal communications, such as by providing a clear process for anyone to report bullying without fear of retaliation. In Chapter 7 we provide scenarios and scripts you can customize for your situation.

Eliminate Us-and-Them Thinking

It's natural for us to hang together in groups of people who are like ourselves, and self-segregation can be a useful coping strategy for minority groups within a dominant culture. We hear a lot these days about how our society has fragmented, and it's easy to identify causes. We are less communal; we often isolate ourselves through the use of social media; there is a lack of agreement about the facts of issues; and we have changed the way we receive news. All these factors reduce our connections with each other and isolate people in camps of Us and Them.

What if instead of focusing on emotions and resentments, you shifted attention to finding better ways to complete your work assignment? What if instead of hanging with people of your same race, social class, gender preference, or religion, you stepped outside of your comfort zone and sought out people who had a similar focus on making the company succeed, and whose professional demeanor and goals matched yours? These would be potential allies as you strive to make positive things happen at work and in your career.

You probably have little choice about who you work with day-to-day, but you can certainly choose who you associate with during lunch and breaks. Could you reach across apparent divides of department, color, and ethnicity? Experts advise people to network outside of their industry to enlarge their scope of connections. You can use the same approach inside your workplace and reach past those you know to explore new connections. If you don't know your coworkers' professional goals, you could ask them or perhaps organize some activities for improving team effectiveness and communication. You might be able to get the company to bring in a consultant for a group activity, or you might guide break-room conversation to get to know each other better.

> Experts advise people to network outside of their industry to enlarge their scope of connections.

Cy Wakeman wrote in *Fast Company* that promoting a "we" culture and building a workplace based on teamwork can help employees redirect their energy away from collusion, assigning blame, and planning defensive moves and toward a workplace that promotes connection, creativity, and productivity. Changing the culture is the best way to change behavior, so focus on your part of the company and see what you can do. That's an excellent way to work through the fear that underlies most hostility, and to help everyone feel respected, admired, valued, and appreciated.

GROW A SUPPORTIVE COMMUNITY

You can work to build a business community with your coworkers by increasing people's sense of belonging and getting them to focus on the business needs and goals you share. Asking for a coworker's ideas and listening to her suggestions, cooperating to meet deadlines, and treating each other with compassion and respect go a long way toward strengthening work relationships. It's a benefit for management, too, because employees become more invested in the work they do and in the company at large. As employees align their business goals, they can work together in new ways, especially if they have helped establish clear policies and procedures that reduce conflict and promote consideration of one another.

"Most sustainable improvements in community occur when citizens discover their own power to act…when citizens stop waiting for professionals or elected leadership to do something, and decide they can reclaim what they have delegated to others," wrote Peter Block, an authority on workplace learning and performance. Individuals have tremendous power to make positive change, especially when they amplify their influence by working together.

Choose Kindness over Popularity

Sometimes the desire to fit in and be liked can lead us to compromise our behavior and agree to things we would not normally accept, including joining the workplace drama around a bully. This is another area where a strong focus on professional goals and your personal boundaries can save you boatloads of grief.

As a general rule, it is better to worry less about joining the pack and more about practicing kindness. Rather than withdraw from the bully into an office clique, what about joining her in the lunch room, asking about the career experiences that brought her to the company, or commenting on a skill she has that you honestly admire. Relating to her as a complete human being might even remove you from the bully's crosshairs. Or not—remember that you can't

> **"It's nice to be important, but it's more important to be nice."**
>
> JOHN TEMPLETON,
> investor and philanthropist

make another person do, think, say, or feel anything, but you *can* change yourself in an instant. You can transform your relationships by changing your expectations and the way you respond. I keep this quote from an unknown author on my desk: "A gentle act of kindness is rarely forgotten."

CULTIVATE RESPECT

It's important to learn to truly listen to other women. Asking what someone thinks is not the same as asking for her to agree with, support, or flatter you. Have you ever perceived a threat from another woman and later found out that no offense was intended? A woman once approached me after a seminar to complain about a young coworker who constantly asked her questions and followed her around. "I think she wants my job!" the woman said. I asked, "Do you think she might be trying to learn from your expertise?" I found out later that the younger woman admired her coworker and was hoping to be mentored. Misunderstandings like this can occur when people assume they know things about each other that are really rooted in fear or unconscious bias.

> Always look for ways to speak your truth clearly, firmly, politely, and without fearing that you will mortally offend or drive away other women.

You also need to step off the gossip train. If you hear complaints from an office bully who dedicates her life to undermining, harassing, and obstructing her coworkers, do not participate. Politely excuse yourself and walk away. Don't succumb to a group mind and behavior that violates your values. Always look for ways to speak your truth clearly, firmly, politely, and without fearing that you will mortally offend or drive away other women. You *must* find ways to fend off insulting behavior without resorting to a nuclear attack. See Chapter 7 for things you can say in situations like this.

"The women I admire…who are successful honor the woman code," wrote author and former White House correspondent Sophia A. Nelson, Esq. expressing her idea of professionalism. "They are collaborators. They don't talk bad about other women. They don't tear other women down. They don't gossip. They don't demean other women. They are too busy being successful for that kind of nonsense, and they don't have time for it. Successful women cultivate and collaborate, and in doing so, they create success."

DIFFICULTIES WITH A WOMAN BOSS

It's good that attention is being paid to bullying at work these days, but it's important to carefully examine what's going on before assuming that you are being bullied. If you feel that your boss is picking on you, consider that she might actually be doing her job by providing useful feedback to help you improve. Women often react negatively to behavior from another woman that they would accept without comment from a man, which is an example of implicit bias in action. No one likes to be criticized, but learning to put down your defensiveness, so you can hear and accept suggestions for improvement, will help you advance quickly. "Rather than an increase in unlawful behavior, we are experiencing an increase in the labelling of difficulties as bullying," Alice DeBoos stated in the article "Is Workplace Bullying on the Rise?" in *Human Resources Director Australia*. Make sure that you are not overreacting to appropriate supervision.

Despite their steadily increasing numbers in upper management, the woman boss remains a favorite villain in watercooler gossip. Nearly 40 percent of women pass along unflattering gossip about their (female) boss, according to a Lifetime Women's Pulse Poll reported by Maxine Rock. This is the opposite of supporting other women and makes no sense. Many people rise in their careers when a boss moves on to a better job and takes a current employee with her, but that's not going to happen if you've been undercutting her. It's better to counteract gossip about your boss or anyone else by expressing your doubts that it's true and suggesting it be confirmed before they repeat it. Gossip hurts everyone, so just don't.

If your boss really *is* the office bully, know that you're not alone. The Workplace Bullying Institute (WBI) reports that 61 percent of bullies are bosses. The boss's position gives her power and she will fight to keep it. She may be an older woman who feels threatened by newcomers or an untrained younger woman insecure in her role. She may be threatened by your abilities or fresh take on a project. Or she may be a deeply unhappy person with a dysfunctional home life that has nothing to do with you. Whatever her motivation, if you act strategically, you can protect your well-being and your career.

A friend of mine worked in an office that was six floors above the rest of her department. In time she acquired a woman supervisor who was new to management and had less education than my friend did. This new supervisor would appear in her office unannounced at odd times during the day, often interrupting meetings. She would look suspicious and ask probing questions, using a tone of "remember who's the boss here." Instead of taking offense, my friend would tell her about the meeting and arrange a time for her to return later. My friend also regularly reassured her insecure supervisor about her authority and kept an eye out for projects that might help the supervisor gain more status in the organization. This strategy reassured the supervisor, who was not even aware of her bullying behavior, and gained my friend an ally.

Treat Women Better

Women have been trained to forgive men almost anything and to thank them for the smallest favor or courtesy. In contrast, women hold other women accountable for the tiniest perceived difference or slight, often jump to criticize each other, can be oversensitive, expect each other to do favors without being asked, and forget to say please and thanks. When Phyllis Chesler conducted interviews for her book *Woman's Inhumanity to Woman*, women "mainly talked about how *other* women had disappointed or betrayed them. Few were able to recall the ways in which *they* had disappointed or betrayed other women." It's *so* much easier to see other people's faults than our own. By becoming aware of our own unconscious biases and intentionally treating all women fairly, we can stop treating other women in ways that infuriate them.

It's *so* much easier to see other people's faults than our own.

Acknowledging our own failings and striving to correct them makes it easier to stop judging other people and increases the likelihood of mutual support. Treating other women warmly and with courtesy helps them feel sincerely appreciated.

If you do feel wronged, sleep on it, and reconsider it carefully after you have calmed down. If someone disagrees with you, it doesn't mean that she is trying to undermine you or has abandoned you or disconnected from you. She is entitled to her opinion, so focus instead on your business goals. After you get clear about what's going on, you might use I-messages (as described in Chapter 7) to express any anger or frustration *one time* directly to the woman with whom you are upset, without mentioning it to anyone else. Then *let go of it.*

WHEN YOU NEED TO WALK AWAY

By analyzing the power structure at work, you can make an educated guess about how likely it is that a bully who is making your life miserable will change or that the company will intervene. Be realistic, because there's no point in wasting your time if the bully has the support of management. If you've tried everything and the bully remains manipulative and unreachable, you may need to walk away, wrote Lindsay Dodgson in *Business Insider.* She paraphrased psychologist Perpetua Neo saying, "Ultimately, the only thing you can do is get as far away from them as possible....You should break away as soon as you know you are with someone who is incapable of empathy and run far away." If you are in a hopelessly toxic situation, focus your efforts on finding your next job ASAP. Picture how great you will feel when this is behind you and new prospects are opening up with a new, better employer and a work group in which you can develop supportive relationships.

The best revenge, Dodgson wrote, "is to live your life, learn from the experience, and grow as a result. Finding out you are stronger and happier without them will help ensure it never happens to you again." This removes the bully's power. "Even though he tried to destroy you, you've turned the tables and instead created an awesome life courtesy of the lessons from what he [or she] did to you," Neo said.

By finding ways to support the humanity of workplace bullies while working to eliminate their toxic behaviors, you may be able to develop more productive, supportive relationships. By working together to support each other's advancement, women can move toward greater equality and opportunity at work and in communities. I believe that's a way to make things better for everyone, so let's keep the positive actions and momentum building. By working and living peacefully, collaboratively, and with profound generosity and kindness, we can create an understanding of one another that allows us to appreciate our strengths and forgive our weaknesses, so we can advance together.

CHAPTER 7

WHAT YOU CAN SAY AND DO

> **"** It's one of the greatest gifts you can give to yourself, to forgive. Forgive everybody. **"**

MAYA ANGELOU, author and activist

Have you ever asked others how they see you? I love hearing people tell me I am a bright light, always positive and uplifting. That makes me feel great because that's how I want to relate to other people. Each of us decides how we show up at work. If what people tell you does not align with how you want to be perceived, you can write a new story by changing your behavior and teaching people to see you differently, as described in Chapter 4 using Carla Harris's advice.

Laurie Battaglia, who helps companies develop engaged, happy team members, told me in our podcast interview that for every consultant who comes in from the outside, there are hundreds of employees who are already changing their company culture from within. Our golden opportunity at work is to be one of those people. This chapter describes challenging workplace scenarios and offers scripts for handling them successfully. Maybe you can modify these approaches to other parts of your life too.

HELP WOMEN ADVANCE

In the first chapter we reported on studies that show that the most effective way to help women advance into management is to have more women on the executive team. The world of finance has been famously dominated by men, so the 2018 selection of Stacey Cunningham as the first-ever woman president of the 226-year-old New York Stock Exchange bodes well for women. There is no better way to end the culture of lack and not-enough that causes relational aggression than by putting more women in management, creating more opportunities, and bringing conflicts out into the open, where they can be resolved.

RESOLVE CONFLICTS WITH CONSTRUCTIVE CONFRONTATION

Years ago I directed a large hospital employee assistance program, which offered management training and consulting to businesses in the area. I learned that too often managers look at employee problems in terms of personality, which makes them impossible to correct. We are who we are, right? Instead, we taught clients to evaluate everything in terms of job performance, and to develop standards for success and criteria for correction.

Eye rolling, for example, is dangerous at work not because the person doing it is a rude person, which isn't really your business, but because it signals disrespect for coworkers and undermines group performance, which *is* your business because you care about your company or organization.

This approach to improving relationships works for ground-level employees as well as managers, and you can even apply it in your personal life (think teenagers), so I'll describe the process. Constructive confrontation techniques (summarized by Tanya Glaser for Beyond Intractability) focus on identifying the cause of the conflict and then curing it. The whole process is grounded in mutual respect to achieve a win-win situation. It's important to remain focused on the process, not the end result, and take one step at a time.

Step 1: Observe Carefully

Be alert for physical mannerisms and indications of indifference, antagonism, or disrespect, which are visible symptoms of a problem:

- Eye rolling
- Avoiding eye contact
- Closed and/or aggressive stance
- Lateness
- Sick a lot—using excessive leave
- Making excuses and blaming others
- Evading or distorting facts
- Telling outright lies
- Inability to understand or accept consequence of actions
- Missing commitments
- Lack of interest or apparent caring
- Petulance or sulking
- Other visible or verbal signs of disrespect

Make specific notes about these behaviors so you can keep the conversation focused on performance. Your goal will be to find out how to align the job with her passion and purpose so that she will engage with the workplace.

Step 2: Discuss the Problem

Once you are clear on the performance issues, bring together the people involved to discuss it. In the first meeting probe for possible misunderstandings and broad problems that are causing conflict, and you may be able to see some positive effects right away.

Step 3: Set Goals Together

Base all goals for improvement on the job description by reviewing it together and connecting the dots with the problem behaviors. In some cases the discussion might include other team members, who might have ideas for solutions and help establish the performance-based goals and deadlines. Set due dates for behavior changes and be specific about how you want people to report their progress.

Continually Ask and Listen

Throughout the process, asking questions is a good way to help empower the person to better understand her relationship to her job and invest in working on the solutions.

- What do you like/dislike about your job?
- What would you change if you could?
- What would make doing your job easier?
- If you need help, what kind of help would be most effective?
- Is there something preventing you from doing your best work?
- What would you like to add to your job if you could?
- Would you change your role in the department (team)? How?

Keep the conversation friendly but firm and build on her answers. Stay focused on the facts, not how she makes you feel. If she is belligerent, stay friendly and composed. Do not take offense no matter what she says, even if she directly criticizes your work style, actions, or behavior. For example, "I appreciate your input and I will think about what you said" is an appropriate response. However, establish your boundaries if she begins to attack your personality: "Let's get back to our relationship here at work so we can both do our jobs better." A manager needs to assert strong boundaries and use her emotional intelligence to remain composed. If things get emotional for either of you, take a break and follow up later: "This has been helpful. Let's take some time to consider what we discussed and meet again to talk more tomorrow."

Problem Solving with Coworkers

In some ways it's easier to apply these techniques among equals because it's a straight collaborative relationship with fewer authority issues. Don't be touchy, keep cool, and focus on gathering the facts. Was something misinterpreted or left undone? What would have helped? Also examine the group dynamics to see who is working well together, who isn't, and what improvements can be made. Do work groups need to be rearranged or lines of communication opened up? Does someone else need to be brought into the group?

Stay out of office politics and remind yourself: Not my drama. Not my circus.

Talk to your coworkers candidly and ask what they think. Every team member can listen to others and accept input openly and constructively. Take the chip off your shoulder, open up to change, and expect a good outcome. Don't assume that you know what others feel or believe. Ask them to tell you. After discussing the issues and agreeing on the changes you wish to see, set a time to revisit the matter and check on progress. Keep your focus on developing smooth performance at work. Constructive confrontation techniques let you figure out what's really going on and devise ways to fix it. Stay out of office politics and remind yourself: Not my drama. Not my circus.

HOW TO COPE WITH MEAN WOMEN

When women leaders are honest about our vulnerabilities and have the courage to ask for help, we open up wonderful opportunities to build alliances and empower our teams. It can be dicey, though, if you have a team member who disrespects others. There is a problem if she:

- Speaks badly of you or anyone else
- Openly snubs someone when he or she speaks to her
- Encourages you to snub someone or suggests that you exclude him or her from a meeting
- Takes you into her confidence, shares secrets, and urges you not to tell
- Has driven people away or people talk about how they *used to be* friends with her

Pay attention if your intuition tells you someone is trying to stir up trouble. Your intuition is almost always correct.

Ask "How Can I Help?"

Suppose you have your dream job except that a coworker is annoying you with tactics like leaving you out of important emails. What could you say or do to get her to stop? Ask for what you want in a non-accusatory way because her behavior really might not be intentional. Face-to-face is best, so try this sample script when talking to the person responsible for communicating with the group:

> *Louise, I need your help. I almost missed last week's staff meeting because I didn't get the email until Sherry forwarded it to me right before the meeting. We all need to be present to meet our challenge. How can we make sure everyone is included in the email?*

Asking how you can help with the situation and seeking advice are two ways to be part of the solution instead of the problem. Don't complain, accuse, or get defensive, and make sure to limit your conversation to one problem. Don't let your thoughts or words stray into other slights or suspected acts of sabotage. Stay on topic: how you can get the next email in a timely fashion.

Any time you have a rocky relationship with someone at your workplace, it may not be about you at all. It could be the person's pending divorce, a family illness, or a matter of timing on your part. Someone else could be pressuring him or her. Until you address it directly and ask for clarification, you won't know the cause of the behavior, so don't assume you do. Assumptions are dangerous because they can cause major kerfuffles. Don't pry into her personal business, but do ask for clarification with a simple I-message:

> *You: Susan, I've fallen off the email list about our task force meetings. Would you please check to be sure I'm included next time?*
> *Susan: Sure.*

You: May I zip you a quick email reminder to check on that?
Susan: Sure.
You: Thank you for your help, Susan.

Handle Passive Aggression

What if the person pretends there is no problem, implies that you're imagining everything or being overly sensitive, and then continues with the slights or passive aggressive behavior? This is annoying, but remember that this is *a performance problem*. It's best to have this discussion privately.

You: Susan, I appreciate the good work you did on [successful project]. I thought you had agreed to provide the reports for [current project] by yesterday afternoon. What happened?
Susan: I didn't get the information.
You: Seriously? I left the paperwork on your desk Tuesday and emailed you the data. I really need that now because our deadline is this afternoon.
Susan: This afternoon? I can't possibly. There's way too much data to enter by then.
You: So you did get the data? I'll see if I Elizabeth can help you so we can meet our deadline. Let's talk later about how we will avoid this kind of problem in the future.

When you catch someone stonewalling or outright lying, move past it to something to achieve actionable results. Don't waste time and energy on dealing with behavior designed to undermine your ability to achieve your goals.

Build a Case to Avoid Getting Fired

In a worst case you may need to gather evidence if someone's ongoing mean behavior threatens your job. Document everything fully: who, what, when, where, and how. Later these files will help you address performance issues of any kind.

- Keep a log at home, not on your work computer, and record incidents and dates as they occur.
- Keep copies of all offending emails and texts (or document the lack of them if you're being cut out of the pipeline).
- Enlist allies, one or more people whom you trust and who have witnessed the relational aggression.
- When you are ready, make an appointment to see the appropriate human resources or leadership team member and request help to alleviate the situation that is keeping you from doing your job. There may be a procedure in place to correct bullying behavior. Experts say that most bosses leave it up to the employees to work it out, but if that has failed, you can use the strategies in Chapter 4 to build your business case, citing facts and figures to show that this performance issue is costing the company money.

Statistics show, unfortunately, that most companies do not act on bullying or relational aggression complaints. If it looks like this is happening in your case, polish up your résumé, kick your networking into high gear, and open your mind to that next job. Knowing that you have options will help you feel calmer and more confident as you move forward.

Persist to Get Results

Diversity expert Dr. Sheila Robinson had been a cheerleader at a Southern high school and, being recognized as the leader that she is, the other cheerleaders wanted her to be their captain. The faculty advisor was deeply prejudiced and didn't want a woman of color as captain, but the squad elected Sheila anyway.

During her tenure as captain the local paper ran a story about the football team and cheerleaders, but the advisor didn't notify Robinson of the photo shoot. She first learned of the article when she saw a photo of the assistant captain, who was white, featured in the paper. It was the first time she had been denied something because of her race.

She channeled her hurt into working with the other cheerleaders to create an award-winning squad that was so good, people attended the football games more to see their routines than to watch the games themselves. Robinson and her team stayed focused on results and they created that success together. Her mantra became: "Succeed in the face of adversity and become an advocate for all women of color."

Support Another Woman Who Is Bullied

I've talked about the group mind that causes people to allow behavior they would never otherwise endorse. I hope that you will turn your negative bullying experience into good by sticking up for others you see being bullied rather than standing idly by. A quiet but firm "Stop tormenting her" or "That's not funny and you know it" makes it clear that you see and reject the bullying behavior. Part of the bully's strategy is to isolate the victim, and the silence of coworkers adds to the victim's despair. You will feel like a hero and—guess what?—you will be!

COMMUNICATE FOR RESULTS

Communication is a hard skill and critical for success, and it needs to be strategic and results-oriented. Be professional, clearly articulate what is going on, and stay focused on the results you want. In many situations relational aggression fades away if you shine a light and talk about it. It really can be that simple. Without pointing a finger, organize a discussion about bullying and its effects at work. Get people talking about their past experience, how it made them feel, what they did to counteract it, and more. At the same time ask your coworkers to write on separate pieces of paper something they admire and appreciate about every member of the work group, including the bully, and give each person their kind words of appreciation.

Communicate Strategically

When you start to feel resentful, always imagine yourself in the other person's shoes and connect with her as a human being. Take responsibility for building a positive relationship, concentrating on your intention for the communication rather than on venting your frustration. Do not accuse the person of anything, and never begin with the word *you*, as in "You are treating me like crap," even though that may be how you're feeling. Develop a strategy for your conversation that will help you learn to communicate with each other more effectively.

You might ask questions like:

- **How are you today?** Moving the focus away from you might actually reveal the reason she is growling at you. Really listen to the answer and refer back to it in your conversation to show that you really listened.
- **Is there something I can do to help you do your job more effectively?** You are not accusing and are ready to accept responsibility for your behavior.
- **Is there a different way you'd like for me to speak with you?** You are reaching out and offering to change in order to smooth your relationship.
- **Please tell me how you'd like for us to work together. I'm having trouble figuring out how to communicate with you.** Offer to make adjustments and be flexible. Listen to her and focus your responses on improving your work relationship.

"Words matter," Marlene Chism wrote on her blog, so stop and think about your language. The more drama we use in our language, the more we create in the workplace, so she urged choosing peace instead. Chism pointed out how language has changed over time: "Language that used to be considered uncivilized and unacceptable has become the norm. It's now common to find social media threads full of vulgarity, verbal assaults, name-calling, and other irresponsible language when people disagree with each other over a political issue or world event." All these tactics increase divisions among people, so avoid them.

Assert Your Boundaries

Establishing your boundaries is fair, reasonable, and necessary. This is assertive behavior, not aggression. The ever-useful I-message works well to share information without making accusations. Tailor this script for your situation:

1. *When you...*(criticize me in front of others, leave me off of important emails, etc.)
2. *I feel...*(embarrassed, angry, frustrated, etc.)
3. *When this happens...*(it's harder for me to do my job, our whole department suffers, etc.)
4. *I'm asking you to...*(give me critiques in private, make a conscious effort to include me in emails, etc.)

If a nasty coworker accuses you of being too sensitive when you deliver your I-message, say, "Perhaps I am too sensitive. However, I'm asking that you discontinue (the unwanted behavior). I appreciate you doing that and feel it will improve our work together." You admit to the sensitivity, focus on the coworker's behavior rather than her personality, ask for a specific action, and express appreciation.

You need to stake out and defend your boundaries because if you allow bullying behavior to continue, it might escalate. Make it clear that you won't become her doormat and remember to always focus on your feelings rather than the other person's actions.

Clearing Up Misunderstandings

No matter how hard you try, communications occasionally go haywire. It's not the end of the world. Use this procedure to reopen conversation in a friendly manner and clear up the confusion.

Set Up Your Meeting
- Plan a strategy beforehand, including the outcome you hope to achieve, without trying to plan the entire conversation, since you can't guess how this person will respond.

- Arrange your chair next to or at a right angle to the other person to establish a sharing relationship rather than a confrontation. This nonverbal communication sets you up "together" rather than in opposition to one another.
- Throughout the conversation actively listen and use the constructive confrontation techniques described earlier in this chapter to figure out what is really behind the problem. Use I-messages to avoid blame and accusation.

Start Talking

- Establish the goal for the communication in your opening statement:

  I'm sorry about our misunderstanding. I truly want to have a positive working relationship with you and want us to understand each other. Can we figure out together how this confusion occurred?

- Describe how you see what happened: *This is how it looked to me.* Then relate the events as you see them without establishing blame. *How did it look to you?*
- Listen and respond, back and forth, always keeping your end goal in mind.
- Strive for agreement or understanding on each point, repeating what you think you heard.
- When you think the misunderstanding has been resolved, agree on actions you will both take to keep this from happening again.
- Schedule a follow-up to check on progress toward your now-shared goal. At that time repeat your intention to develop a positive relationship and express how you appreciate the other person's willingness to work on it with you.

Few misunderstandings are so great that you have to bring in someone else to help you unravel the problem. If you map out a clear strategy, establish the objectives clearly in the beginning, speak honestly, and get an authentic response from the other person, you should be able to mend fences yourself.

Reopening a Difficult Conversation

Sometimes you end a negotiation or conversation and wish later for a different outcome. Think carefully about the outcome you desire, and reopen the discussion like this:

> *SuLynn, I appreciated our conversation and realize it's not settled yet for me. Are you willing to talk with me about it a little more? We need to both feel comfortable with our solution.*

Calmly state the issue that is not completed for you yet, and talk through the remaining problems.

Follow the procedure in the previous "Clearing Up Misunderstandings" example until you reach the conclusion you hoped for. Remember to agree on steps to prevent further miscommunication and set a follow-up meeting to confirm that you have *both* done what you agreed you would do.

Responding to Criticism

Suppose a vice president criticizes you about something you missed.

- Do not blame anyone, especially your boss. Even if the vice president was at fault and didn't tell you that you were supposed to do something, don't blame her or him directly. Apologize and offer to fix the problem or provide the service in a prompt manner.
- Focus language on the future and how to achieve positive outcomes. Keep it results-oriented.
- If it's not in your power to act alone or lead a team to fill the void, offer a plan with the caveat that you will run it by your management.

- If a member of your team dropped the ball, follow the same guidelines and keep your language performance-based. State the problem clearly and ask questions about the action you thought you had assigned.
  - Did the employee have it on her schedule?
  - Did she get tied up elsewhere?
  - What can she do to provide the service or fix the problem?

Stay focused on the solution, not the mistake. Ignore it if she tries to blame someone else (or you), and avoid finding fault or threatening punishment. Ask for alternatives and allow the person who made the mistake to participate in solving the problem. Often, ground-level employees have good ideas for improvement, but no one ever asks for or listens to their opinions.

HOW TO HEAL A TOXIC CULTURE

If you're working or managing in a top-down dominating workplace, it might be difficult to change the culture from within. However, you can make clear to your group how much you value them and how important you all are to each other's performance. Knowing that others depend on you is a great motivator for people to do their best work, feel like they belong, and take responsibility for the results. Develop the mantra, *When you're okay, I'm okay. When you're not okay, neither am I.* You will be happier at work if your attitude encourages mutual support and working together as interdependent members of the work community.

In Chapter 2 we mentioned Maggie Castro-Stevens's annoyance when people assume things about her because she is Latina. People may say she is being oversensitive when their biased assumptions offend her, but she replies, "Don't blow it off as if it's not important; it's important to me. If it's important to me, it should be important to you. If we're working in a collaboration together, it's important to the outcome of the project."

Collaboration is the key because it gets everyone working—together—on the same side of the problem. An atmosphere of collaboration, camaraderie, and trust develops personal and professional responsibility in every group member. Interestingly, this sense of responsibility can encourage a coworker who hasn't been a team player to become one, because she feels an obligation to the group.

> Knowing that others depend on you is a great motivator for people to do their best work, feel like they belong, and take responsibility for the results.

To build a team mentality, volunteer to help ensure that the rules apply equally to all employees. Kim can't be allowed to come in late because she has childcare issues while Linda, who has no kids, gets docked for missing the bus. Even the CEO should be at her desk on time if it's a company rule for others. If your company's policies and procedures manual is outdated, pull together a committee and fix it. If the company doesn't have such a manual, volunteer to work with others to create one.

Get Permission to Set Up a Committee

It's fair to say that most managers and owners often feel overwhelmed by all they have to do, and they won't appreciate you trying to change the system or adding to their burdens. However, if you can identify coworkers who are willing to work on solutions with you and present the business case for your idea, you will be more likely to get permission.

You: Ms. Henderson, several of us have noticed confusion among our coworkers about the attendance policies at our company. Not *everyone follows the same rules. People feel resentful and spend a lot of time talking about it.*

<u>Ms. Henderson:</u> *Yes, I've noticed that too.*

<u>You:</u> *I think we would be more productive if we had a simple policies and procedures manual to tell everyone what the rules are. Grace and Lester are interested in helping to draft something for your review. Would you authorize us to work as a committee?*

<u>Ms. Henderson:</u> *We're too busy and I don't want you taking time away from your work.*

<u>You:</u> *We have talked about that and know this will save you money. We each need to spend an hour of research time. Our eight coworkers each spend five minutes a day arguing, complaining, and thinking about attendance and lateness. Having clear policies and procedures would eliminate that, and the productive time they gain will pay for all our research time after just two weeks.*

<u>Ms. Henderson:</u> *It would be great not to hear all that griping. Okay, go ahead as long as you can still meet our project deadlines.*

<u>You:</u> *Will do. We will show you a draft in two weeks.*

De-Escalate Tensions

If you need to de-escalate tensions in your group, breathe deeply, pause, and separate the facts from the feelings before you respond. If there is any possibility of violence, make sure to develop a plan for security with a manager and have another person present in the meeting.

Focus on making your breathing deep and even before you speak. Take at least a couple of minutes if you can. Then try using statements and questions like these:

- "I admire the work you do to help our work group succeed. Have I done something to make you unhappy with me? I feel a weird vibe that makes me uncomfortable."
- "I want to have a good working relationship with you. What ideas do you have for improving the way we work together?"

- "I can see that you're upset, but when you talk to me in that manner, I feel offended. Let's stop now and pick up another time."
- "You raised some very interesting points. I'd like to take a break to think about this. Can we meet to discuss this again tomorrow afternoon?"

Practice Persistent Kindness

If you have a toxic culture at your workplace, you can do your part to systematically transform it. Be persistent and reach out with kindness and open, transparent professionalism. Mean what you say. Don't be fake or superficial. If you can't be real, it's better not to engage. You and your coworkers all have the power to:

- Find out what other coworkers' interests are
- Share something, perhaps an article they might be interested in
- Invite a colleague to a coffee break (maybe offer to buy this time)
- Be open about your intentions to advance, perhaps by asking an older colleague how she developed her career
- See colleagues as people and really listen to what they say
- Really see them and show appreciation if they do something well, especially when they help you
- Always be kind, even though they may not be

See an Abundance of Goodness

A wonderful remedy for many workplace challenges is to reach out and help others. I found that women are often shocked when I offer to help them. But that is what we must do. Gloria Feldt will never forget the way her boss, Mildred, took the time to write a recommendation from her deathbed. That generous gesture changed the trajectory of Feldt's entire life.

Small gestures can make an enormous difference for another woman. Similarly, sales trainer Judy Hoberman has set a goal to help one woman every day. This approach builds a supportive culture because each time you help another person advance, you show you believe in her, which builds her confidence. Everyone who has accomplished anything at all in life had at least one person who told them that they are worthy, they have value and talent, and they can succeed. These generous gestures expand like ripples on a pond.

A wonderful remedy for many workplace challenges is to reach out and help others.

Most people will want to help you if you remember to ask, "Will you help me?" Then return the favor by offering, "How can I help you?"

Raise Expectations So Women See What's Possible

When women feel hopeless at work, they don't work for change. Women supporting each other enables us to focus on the values we believe in, visualize the world we want to create, and amplify our power by working together. "When women see a real possibility for change, they seize it," Dr. Judith Rodin, president of the Rockefeller Foundation, and Monique Villa, CEO of the Thomson Reuters Foundation, wrote in *HuffPost*. "They find the courage, and are more likely to speak up, demanding—and often obtaining—fairer treatment and equal opportunities. On the contrary, where expectations are low, women tend to remain silent, as they perceive inequality as part of the status quo." Rodin reported a study of the G20 countries that looked at progress toward equal wages and against sexual violence in India. Once the conversation about the issues started, women came forward and told their stories and changed things for the better.

When women speak up in conversations about things that matter, our shared hope and determination for change alter how women *feel* about their environments. When we shift our perceptions, share our stories, work together, and concentrate on improving things for everyone, we can make big changes. Women act on their beliefs. If we believe that we can change things for the better, women can move heaven and earth. The best way to gain equality and take our full 50 percent share of leadership is to believe that we can, and that our actions will make the world a better place for everyone.

Stay Open to Opportunity

Things can change in surprising ways, so why not expect the best? You might go around a barrier or turn an opponent into an ally, or sometimes the barrier evaporates on its own. Dr. Sheila Robinson told a story with a surprise ending that proves you never know what might happen. A white supervisor, who was a man, once told her that she would never advance at their company. He had much more power than she, so Robinson assumed she should start searching for a different job. But before she had the chance, her supervisor moved on. Her new manager recognized Robinson's potential and pushed her forward in team meetings and offered new opportunities. Robinson set records with the company, getting a promotion each year for five years, and ending up working with a global marketing team. She could not have predicted that outcome at the start.

The person who is troubling you might move on, but in the meantime be alert for improvements you can make yourself. The important thing here is not to let barriers defeat you. Set a strategy; go over, around, or through. Stay focused on the results you want, gather your team, and be the leader of your life and career.

BUILD A CULTURE OF GRATITUDE

If being kind and thoughtful is not part of your company's culture, you can be the first to make a change. Other people may question your intentions, but keep it up and you can wear them down. It's impossible to ignore kindness that is authentically and generously given over time. At some point others might join you.

"People can't help but pay gratitude forward," wrote Louisa Kamps in reference to the work of Robert Emmons, a pioneer of gratitude research. "When appreciation is expressed, it triggers a biological response in the recipient's brain, including a surge of the feel-good chemical dopamine." Expressing gratitude toward a colleague makes her feel grateful in return. "What's more, thanking your benefactors makes them feel good about the kind acts that they've done, so they want to continue doing them, not only for you but also for others."

The most productive and pleasant places to work are those where everyone feels valued and respected, which makes them eager to contribute all of their talent and energy to achieve the organization's goals. When women support other women and work together with their "power to," everyone wins. Reach out to a woman who least expects it; perhaps you can make an ally of a former competitor. Imagine the difference you could make if you worked on it together.

Part 3

ELIMINATING HARASSMENT AND VIOLENCE

The war between the sexes drives the plot of many a movie and novel, but it drains far too much energy from our families, businesses, and communities. We think it's time to stop it. The #MeToo and #TimesUp campaigns reflect a sharp decrease in tolerance of sexual assault and harassment, which have long been used to keep women down. We'll talk about the ways our culture trains men to scorn and abuse women, a behavior pattern that takes a heavy toll at work and at home.

Our internal biases (in women and men) define what we dare to aspire to and keep us from supporting each other's advancement. Many layers make up the uneasy and conflicted relationships between men and women, and we will unpack the issues to look at how we can understand and change them. We touch on ways that women can recruit male allies to the cause of equality and work with supportive men to correct the system that pits us against each other. This section closes with strategies for engaging male allies and sample scripts for talking about these issues. We all have so much to gain if we can work side by side—together.

CHAPTER 8
LET'S END SEXUAL HARASSMENT

❝We do not need magic to change the world. We carry all the power we need inside ourselves already. We have power to imagine better.❞

J.K. ROWLING, author

In late 2017 Tarana Burke, founder of the organization Just Be Inc., which helps victims of sexual harassment and assault, saw her decade-old "Me Too" slogan go viral when it was tweeted in hashtag form by actress Alyssa Milano. Suddenly and swiftly a movement of women began supporting each other as never before and an important reckoning began. Women in the entertainment industry talked publicly about ways their careers and their personal lives had been negatively affected by sexual harassment from powerful men at some of the world's largest media and entertainment companies. Before long women in every industry and from every country began calling out their assailants, saying, "Enough." Women no longer felt isolated, and it became clear that these high-profile stories were just the tip of the iceberg.

This is not an attack on all men but is instead a group of women calling out those who have harmed them, and demanding change in a system that, until recently, has failed them. Women from all walks of life are rising up in solidarity to support one another's courage in speaking out about being harassed, catcalled, groped, and raped. These women broke their silence, and by talking about their experiences in the workplace and in their communities, they are helping other women do the same. The success of women calling out harassment and violence after the fact in no way minimizes the suffering inflicted by violent men on millions of people all over the world. It's progress, yes, but our goal is to prevent this behavior, so women are no longer hurt.

COMPLICATED HUMAN RELATIONSHIPS

People have lots of mixed feelings about other genders. This makes our relationships messy and confusing. In describing the typical relationships between men and women, sociologist Peter Glick noted the ambivalent interdependence that marks human intimate partner relationships. This is different than codependence and means that, as independent adults, we rely on one another to fulfill our social and emotional needs for friendship, communication, nurturing, appreciation, and learning. Intimate partners also fulfill sexual needs.

Our culture has long taught men to take out their frustrations on the women in their lives, with disastrous consequences. That said, it's still reasonable to believe that sexual harassment and violence will continue to decrease over time, especially in light of women's increasing solidarity with each other and with supportive men, and today's increasingly public conversations.

SEX AND GENDER

In Chapter 2 I discussed numerous studies showing that women's and men's behavior is far more alike than different, with these exceptions: cisgender men are typically bigger and stronger and more interested in casual sex. Considering that strength and interest, it's no surprise that women have always dealt with sexual harassment and assault. I'm not saying, "Oh, that's just men; what can you do?" No. It's not. Most men do not commit sexual assault, nor do they intend to harass. Experts point out that motives are varied and include a desire to exert power over women, as Heather Murphy wrote in her 2017 *New York Times* article "What Experts Know about Men Who Rape." If we are to end sexual harassment and violence, we need to understand what it is, what it is not, and how to combat it. Although most men do not rape or harass women, neither do most men feel a responsibility to stop others from doing so.

I do believe that a high percentage of unwelcome, harassing comments are a result of adolescent awkwardness, thoughtlessness, or not knowing what to say. That means we need to teach men how to treat women. It is time for women to insist that men share the responsibility when it comes to stopping other men from committing assault and abuse. This is *not* a women's problem. It's a human problem, and that means that all of us need to work together to move civilization another giant step forward.

It is time for women to insist that men share the responsibility when it comes to stopping other men from committing assault and abuse. This is *not* a women's problem. It's a human problem.

A male friend said years ago, "Women taught us men how to be sensitive because they wouldn't have sex with us if we were not." I believe that most men actually do want to learn how to please women, and together, now that they are listening, we can teach them. See Chapter 10 for ways to approach those who are ready to learn. As for the men who refuse to learn and persist in assaulting women, they belong in jail.

An early Greek comic playwright, Aristophanes, wrote a famous play in which women ended a war by refusing to have sex with their partners until they stopped fighting. It was first performed in 411 B.C.E. Much more recently, in Liberia in 2005, social worker and peace activist Leymah Gbowee helped lead a group of women who, in just over a year, ousted a murderous dictator, ended a fourteen-year war, and elected the first woman president. They brought Christian and Muslim women together; used work strikes, nonviolent protest, song, and prayer; and threatened a sex strike until the war stopped. Sex shouldn't be part of the workplace, of course, but it's certainly part of most women's lives. In this case, Liberian women used the threat of a sex strike—and the resultant publicity—to draw international media attention, which attracted United Nations attention, focused peace keeper energy on the country's plight, and brought about major changes.

Keep in mind that women harass and assault men too. Women can and do exhibit predatory sexual behavior, and the men who speak out are often discounted or shamed as much as women. One in six complaints with the US Equal Employment Opportunity Commission (EEOC) this decade was filed by a man. Interestingly, though, people perceive coercive behaviors by men as aggressive, while those same actions by women are interpreted as romantic and seductive, even though that's not how such behaviors feel to the men on the receiving end. Regardless of your gender, unwanted touching is not sexy; it's assault. Uninvited actions are, more often than not, unwanted.

RECOGNITION OF HARASSMENT AS A CRIME

The idea that men do not have the right to treat women any way they want (at work or anyplace else) is quite new. Sexual harassment was first defined as an illegal form of sex discrimination in the Civil Rights Act of 1964 and again in Title IX, which is a federal civil rights law passed as part of the Education Amendments of 1972. Stalking wasn't criminalized until California did so in 1990, and the other forty-nine states took years to follow suit. Federal regulations require most colleges and universities to develop formal sexual harassment policies and grievance procedures, and many businesses and organizations have them also, yet these often do not help women. The employee assistance program I directed in the 1990s helped companies write policies and procedures defining sexual harassment, and I learned that it was often more about power and control than sexual desire.

Now that these offenses are finally gaining some legal standing, we need procedures for reviewing the evidence, and a structure that clearly defines the degree and nature of the offenses. Let me be clear: I think it's right to punish a malicious harasser, and I fully support women speaking out at last. But it's not fair to fire someone who is just an awkward fool. Yes, he absolutely needs to be made to stop his abusive behaviors, but I don't see the benefit of ending someone's career because he made a stupid adolescent joke.

#MeToo Times Twelve Million

While working quietly to support survivors of sexual assault, activist Tarana Burke developed the organization MeToo more than a decade ago. Imagine her surprise in the aftermath of the Harvey Weinstein accusations to see #MeToo used online more than twelve million times, and to find herself on the red carpet at the Golden Globes along with seven other women's rights activists and some very glamorous movie stars. When actress Michelle Williams invited Burke to be her guest at the Golden Globes, she responded, "Why? I'm trying very hard not to be the black woman who is trotted out when you all need to validate your work." They came to an understanding, though, and Burke said the evening was an indication of "how women have historically supported each other."

Burke made an important point about our culture's shift toward greater support for women. "I don't think that every single case of sexual harassment has to result in someone being fired," she said. "The consequences should vary. But we need a shift in culture so that every single instance of sexual harassment is investigated and dealt with. That's just basic common sense."

Small Abuses Enable Larger Abuses

"There is a spectrum of abuse," wrote Gretchen Kelly in a *Facebook* post on The Good Men Project's #StopSexism Social Interest Group. "Not all abuse is equal. But the important thing to remember is that the smaller abuses feed and enable the larger abuses. In some cases, the permissibility of the smaller abuses emboldens men to commit the more violent abuses. That's why we should have a no tolerance policy. The way we address these abuses is up for discussion. But minimizing them is only aiding rape culture." She included a pyramid graphic showing the systematic progression of the levels of abuse: normalization (locker room talk, victim blaming), degradation (catcalling, stalking, unsolicited "dick pics"), removal of autonomy (groping, sexual coercion, drugging), and explicit violence (rape, molestation).

Sexual Harassment Definitions

I hope and expect that such cases will receive increasing attention as we work to stop and define punishments for the abuses, so let's look quickly at the legal definitions of coercion, unwanted sexual attention, or gender harassment. The EEOC defines workplace sexual harassment as unwelcome sexual advances or conduct of a sexual nature that unreasonably interferes with the performance of a person's job or creates an intimidating, hostile, or offensive work environment. Sexual harassment can range from persistent, offensive, sexual jokes to inappropriate touching to posting offensive material on a bulletin board.

While Title VII of the 1964 Civil Rights Act serves as a baseline for sexual harassment claims, many states have laws in place that may be stricter. Under Title VII there are two recognized types of sexual harassment:

- **Quid pro quo** (which in Latin means "this for that") is a form of harassment where a person in authority, usually a supervisor, demands that subordinates tolerate harassment as a condition of getting or keeping a job or benefit, including promotions and raises. Just one instance of harassment is sufficient to sustain a quid pro quo claim.

- **Hostile environment** harassment is grounds for legal action when the conduct is unwelcome, sexual in nature, and severe enough to create an abusive or offensive work environment. The courts usually analyze:
  - Whether the conduct was verbal, physical, or both
  - The frequency of the conduct
  - If the conduct was hostile or patently offensive
  - Whether the alleged harasser was a coworker or supervisor
  - Whether others joined in perpetuating the harassment
  - If the harassment was directed at more than one person or singled out the victim

The burden typically falls on the victim to prove the claim, and she has historically run the risk of demotion, unemployment, and ridicule.

Is It Harassment?

Many women are not certain that what is happening to them actually constitutes harassment. Women have been so conditioned to serve men's agendas, and the penalties for making an accusation can be so severe, that they doubt themselves at every turn. If you are unsure, review the definition of workplace sexual harassment given earlier in this chapter and ask someone you trust outside of your organization. Be aware that in many organizations, unfortunately, the HR department's purpose is to protect the interests of the organization, not yours. If you or someone you know may be subject to harassment, insist that other women listen and offer support to make it stop. At work the perpetrator of quid pro quo harassment usually has more power than his target, including control over a job, a promotion, perks, or benefits that the target needs.

TOXIC MASCULINITY

Toxic masculinity occurs with an adherence to traditional male gender roles that restrict the emotions boys and men are allowed to express. This includes expectations that men dominate others, especially women, and suppress expressions of any emotion other than anger. Clearly this limits men's ability to express their humanity. Even as women represent a larger and larger percentage of the workforce, most workplace cultures remain more masculine than balanced. In fact, Anne Hardy, at the time a vice president of technology strategy at SAP Labs, was quoted in *Knowledge@Wharton* as saying that companies today "are building on masculine norms." Managers should try to create business environments in which women can "thrive and grow," and where they can feel welcomed and encouraged.

Women business leaders agree that the workplace would probably function differently—with a very different look and feel—if it were built by and for women. The more women are present, the less vulnerable they become, even in workplaces dominated by men where harassers try to show women who is boss.

These behaviors don't start in the workplace; they are learned at home, in the community, and even in school. Jennifer Siebel Newsom, wife of the lieutenant governor of California and the mother of two sons, premiered her film *The Mask You Live In* at the Sundance Film Festival in 2015. She maintains that our hypermasculine culture encourages violence. Her film documents American stereotyping of men into a narrow definition of masculinity, and shows how our culture trains men to think that they are entitled and women are inferior, a process that harms men and boys too.

Reaction to Rejection

Rejection is painful for anyone, and many men do not handle it well. Case in point, twenty-two-year-old Elliot Rodger killed six people in a drive-by shooting in Santa Barbara County in 2014. As reported by the BBC, he left behind a *YouTube* video in which he vowed revenge on women, mentioning that he'd never had an intimate experience. The tragedy led to an important conversation and initiated the #YesAllWomen campaign. The basis of the campaign is that all women have experienced gender-based violence despite the fact that not all men have committed acts of violence. Since the incident women have been sharing stories about the abuse they have faced after rejecting sexual advances from men, thereby shining light on this difficult subject.

Rodger expressing his rage at his lack of romantic success with women is an extreme example of entitlement, which may be expressed at work by anger at a woman who gets "my job" or "my promotion." Some men feel that they are entitled to their position of authority and the privilege of power, which causes them to resent and resist women seeking equal power. They may also feel that they are owed sexual gratification and have the right to punish any woman for perceived slights.

This sense of entitlement can be compounded in the workplace, especially in cultures dominated by men, and it's important for men to realize that they are not entitled to any woman's affection, time, conversation, or body—no matter what. It does not matter whether she is his subordinate or superior, whether he hired her or gave her a raise, a woman does not "owe" him *anything*.

Bro Culture

One offshoot of the hypermasculine culture is the "bro culture," a younger men's subculture of conventional "guys' guys" who spend time together partying. Although the popular image of the bro lifestyle is associated with sports apparel and fraternities, as these men grow up and take jobs, it is emerging in the workplace, primarily in tech.

This culture led Loretta Lee, who worked at Google from 2008 to 2016, to file a suit for sexual harassment, gender discrimination, and wrongful termination in California state court. In the complaint Lee alleged "that she was subject to 'lewd comments, pranks and even physical violence' on a daily basis, including having male colleagues spike her drinks with alcohol, shoot Nerf balls at her, send her sexually suggestive messages and, in one case, slap her in the face," according to an article by Julia Carrie Wong in *The Guardian*.

Lee was especially upset when she found a male coworker on all fours beneath her desk and "believed he may have installed some type of camera or similar device under her desk," the complaint stated. The suit alleged that Google's treatment of Lee was "consistent with a pattern and practice of ignoring sexual harassment in the workplace, making no significant efforts to take corrective action, and punishing the victim." Lee's is the latest in a string of lawsuits that have targeted the company over workplace issues involving harassment, speech, and diversity.

WHO ENCOUNTERS SEXUAL HARASSMENT AT WORK?

The number of women who have experienced sexual harassment is staggering, although it's difficult to find consistent data. According to a poll by *ABC News* and *The Washington Post*, reported by Gary Langer, 54 percent of American women said they have experienced unwanted and inappropriate sexual advances in life, and nearly a third have encountered them at work. In contrast, studies by the US Equal Employment Opportunity Commission found that up to 85 percent of women have experienced sexual harassment in the workplace and that three-fourths of sexual harassment victims never report it. A 2014 study from the Restaurant Opportunities Centers United, cited on the Rave Mobile Safety website by Jackson Lucas, reported that 66 percent of female restaurant employees reported having been sexually harassed by managers, with more than half saying it happened at least once a week. The same study found that over 50 percent of women in tipped occupations reported that their dependence on tips led to acceptance of inappropriate behavior that made them nervous or uncomfortable. None of these studies addressed the race or ethnicity of the affected employees.

Women employed in majority-male workplaces are more likely to say that their gender has made it harder for them to get ahead at work, wrote Kim Parker in a Pew Research Center report. They are also less likely to say that women there are treated fairly in personnel matters, and they report experiencing gender discrimination at significantly higher rates. Disappointingly, nearly a third of women who work in mostly female workplaces say the same.

Race and Harassment

Actress Salma Hayek talked at the Cannes Film Festival about the abuse she experienced from Harvey Weinstein while making *Frida* in 2002, and about his reaction to her charges. "He only responded to two women, two women of color," Hayek said, the other being Lupita Nyong'o. "It was a strategy by the lawyers, because we are the easiest to get discredited. It is a well-known fact, if you are a woman of color, people believe what you say less. So he went attacking the two women of color, in hopes that if he could discredit us, he could then maybe discredit the rest." This intersectionality of race and gender leaves women of color more vulnerable to harassment than white women. Although the vast majority of rapes are reported by white women, according to university campus data, women of color are more likely to be assaulted and victimized by violent crime than white women.

> It is a well-known fact, if you are a woman of color, people believe what you say less.

In fact, a 2010 study on sexual violence by the Centers for Disease Control and Prevention (CDC) "found that 4 out of 5 women who said they had experienced attempted or a completed rape in their lifetime identified as a non-white woman of color," reported Jackson Lucas for Rave Mobile Safety. Not only are women of color and women in marginalized communities more likely to be victims of assault, but they also face more hurdles when they come forward. Writing for the *Catalyst Blog*, Katherine Giscombe, PhD, pointed out a double standard for prosecuting assailants of whites and women of color. While minority women suffer assault at higher rates, Dr. Giscombe reported that a Brandeis University study found huge discrepancies in how the perpetrators were prosecuted. "In one locality, researchers found that prosecutors filed charges in 75% of the cases in which a White woman was attacked, but when the victim was a Black woman, prosecutors filed charges just 34% of the time."

During an interview, *PBS NewsHour* reporter Hari Sreenivasan reminded Tarana Burke of her earlier comment, "Sexual violence doesn't see race or class, but the response to it does." Dr. Giscombe explained the historical reference that allows such wholesale abuse of women of color, from Latinas as part of European colonization, to Asians as spoils of war and the sexualization of women as geishas, and black women often being stripped to show their attributes when sold as slaves. Combine this with the masters using sex to demoralize women slaves to keep them in their place and you have the foundation for today's treatment of women of color in the workplace. Dr. Giscombe urges women to find unity across the diversity of women and view the experiences of women of color the same way we view those of white women. We must create a united front of understanding and compassion and stand firm to "gain the strength to effectively overcome oppression."

Abuse of Low-Wage Earners

"The customer is always right" dominates the restaurant and hospitality industries. That mantra and the imbalance of economic power between the perpetrators of sexual harassment and their victims, especially when their victims are working at near poverty, keep women fearful and quiet. In 2016 the labor union Unite Here surveyed around 500 of its Chicago-area members who worked in hotels and casinos as housekeepers and servers, many of whom are Latino and Asian immigrants. Among the results, reported by Dave Jamieson in *HuffPost*, 58 percent of hotel workers said that they had been sexually harassed by a guest, and 49 percent said that a guest had answered the door naked or otherwise exposed himself. Maria Elena Durazo, a labor leader with the union, said, "Frankly, I don't think much of the public understands what housekeepers go through just to clean these rooms and carry out the work." For several years Durazo's union has advocated for panic buttons as part of the employment contracts. Now they have received approval and backing from the city of Chicago to make it a citywide requirement. Chicago was the second city to institute the system. Seattle was the first. This costly move wouldn't be necessary, Durazo said, if we would change the culture. "We have to do something to equalize the power so that women really have the ability to speak up, without having to risk their livelihood…whether you're a housekeeper or a food server or a big-time actor."

Abuse of Athletes

In September 2015 physician Larry Nassar abruptly retired from USA Gymnastics with little fanfare. By May 16, 2018, about three hundred young women and one man had accused him of sexual assault, according to a *Vox* article by Jen Kirby. The highly disciplined athletes had been trained to accept without question the training routines prescribed by male coaches, and when they began to complain, the Olympic establishment ignored their concerns. The young women persisted, and in January 2018, after seven days of survivors' statements, a judge ordered Nassar to serve up to 175 years in prison.

Six-time Olympic medalist Aly Raisman spent months urging the US Olympic Committee and USA Gymnastics to investigate Nassar's abusive conduct and demanded answers as to why it was allowed to continue for so long. Frustrated by the lack of progress, Raisman filed a lawsuit against both organizations, claiming they "knew or should have known" about Nassar's abusive pattern of behavior. Hers is one of more than one hundred civil actions filed against Nassar and USA Gymnastics, prompted by lack of confidence that Olympic games institutions were doing enough to stop it. It's highly likely that many less famous women pursuing athletic careers experience abuse as well. Raisman contends that, "Without a solid understanding of how this happened, it is delusional to think sufficient changes can be implemented." Young athletes' determination to stand up for each other and their refusal to remain silent have been entirely responsible for prompting action in this dark area of abuse.

Harassment in the Military

The less power and status a woman can claim, the more likely she is to fall victim to sexual assault—a common male response to women entering domains dominated by men, like the military and firefighting. Suicide rates among female veterans are double those of civilian women and have been increasing more rapidly than suicide rates in other vets, according to Jack Moore writing in *Newsweek*. "Women are more likely than men to experience instances of sexual harassment, sexual discrimination and rape in the military and the resultant mental health issues, or what female US military vet Letrice Titus called 'military sexual trauma.'" Assaults in the military disproportionately affect women of color, who, according to Statista, make up more than 48 percent of female enlistees, despite comprising 38 percent of the population in the US.

The military has been working to reduce those rates as the number of women in service increases and they gain more status. According to the 2014 RAND Military Workplace Study, reported by Jim Garamone, the percentage of active duty women who experienced unwanted sexual contact in the previous year declined from 6.1 percent in 2012 to an estimated 4.3 percent in 2014. A drop of nearly one third in two years would be good news, but there are systemic issues that call into question the numbers provided by the military. The military chain of command requires a soldier to file a complaint with her commanding officer, who in many cases is the assailant, pointed out PBS *Frontline*'s Sarah Childress. This reporting system is as flawed as that of a company where a harassing boss is the head of the HR department.

A 2017 media advisory on the website of the Service Women's Action Network noted that almost a third of women reported military sexual trauma during their service as the largest negative influence on their mental health, and nearly half had been negatively affected by gender bias, sexual harassment, and/or sexual violence.

British and Canadian militaries have already addressed the problem by removing assault complaints from the chain of command, but the US Senate blocked such a bill in 2014. Senator Kirsten Gillibrand has introduced a bill proposing that change every year since then and continues to work to build support for it. The fear of sexual assault clearly continues to restrict women's independence and opportunity, so this is another area where having more women in power will help enable positive change. As efforts to elect more women legislators succeed, and as women pressure male elected officials to support such laws, these changes will occur more quickly.

LGBTQ+ Harassment

Members of the LGBTQ+ communities may experience even higher levels of harassment and assault than straight and cisgender women. This is the result of the power dynamics described earlier. The more agency an individual's identity gives them in society, the safer they are. Queer women, especially transgender women of color, are most vulnerable to sexual violence because others act out their entitlement and rage on them simply for existing. Citing Out & Equal, Ariel Sobel reported in *The Advocate* that one of every four LGBTQ employees has experienced discrimination in the past five years, and 10 percent have left a job because the environment was hostile. People have faced harassment, discipline, or termination for wearing their wedding rings at work or having attended gay-lesbian social events. They are mocked or taunted, receive threats, are passed over for promotions, receive unfair evaluations, and are denied benefits. One boss told their trans employee not to mention or praise the company's (progressive) nondiscrimination policy around other employees because it made them feel uncomfortable.

Electing members of these communities to public office is essential to gaining better representation. In 2017 Andrea Jenkins became the first openly transgender black woman elected to public office when she won a seat on the Minneapolis City Council. In the same election cycle Danica Roem of the Virginia House of Delegates won the first seat in a US state legislature to be held by an openly transgender person. Kyrsten Sinema, who has served in both chambers of the Arizona state legislature and in the US House of Representatives, is seeking a US Senate seat in 2018. If elected, Sinema would become the first openly bisexual person elected to the US Senate and the second openly LGBTQ+ person ever to serve in Congress, after Tammy Baldwin.

HOW SEXUAL HARASSMENT AT WORK USED TO BE HANDLED

In the not-so-distant past it was widely assumed, if not expected, that the boss might make a pass at his secretary. Mothers would advise their daughters, "Honey, that's just life" or, if the harassment was really bad, "Go find another job."

The documentary film *Seeing Allred*, directed by Roberta Grossman and Sophie Sartain, tells the story of the famous women's rights attorney Gloria Allred and reflects the progress made in the journey of exposing sexual violence and harassment. In the film, Mariann Meier Wang, a civil rights attorney and New York co-counsel at Allred's firm, said that thirty or forty years ago women were counseled to say nothing more about it and just cry privately.

Allred changed that standard by aggressively staging press conferences in which the woman owned the narrative and was able to speak the truth as she experienced it. "Although critics might say its tawdry, it's rude, it's embarrassing, it allows the public to see what happens in the dark and to see the abuse that often occurs in secret," stated Wang in the documentary.

In the film, Allred described being raped at gunpoint by a physician while on a vacation in Mexico in her twenties. "I thought, who's going to believe me against a doctor?" she recalled. Continuing with her story, she said she was impregnated by that rape and had a back-alley abortion, where she almost died. She developed a very high fever, hemorrhaged, and ended up in the hospital packed in ice. This was before Roe v. Wade legalized abortion in the US, and Allred said that a nurse told her, "This will teach you a lesson." Gloria took this horrible negative experience and turned it into a positive. Summarizing the impact of this experience in the documentary, she said, "It helps me to understand others, and I have represented many women who have been survivors of violence against them, of rape, of child sexual abuse." She shares her own process of recovery "to tell people how to evolve from being a victim, to becoming a survivor, to becoming a fighter for change."

Not only are antiquated gender biases still prevalent at work, but sexual harassment is also still widespread, and unfortunately many women still feel compelled to accept the abuse. The women who have spoken out have started crucial conversations, though, and it's exciting to see the power of women hearing, supporting, and amplifying each other's voices. The spotlight on sexual harassment at work today emphasizes the illegality of men's actions and the toll this has taken on women's advancement. This is happening because more women have risen through the ranks at work and are using their hard-won influence to help each other be heard.

HOW SEXUAL HARASSMENT AT WORK IS HANDLED TODAY

A *Time*/SurveyMonkey poll suggested that people believe that women are much more likely to speak out about harassment since the Weinstein allegations, according to Charlotte Alter. In the past women who came forward were too often ignored or shamed and discredited, so that means women have a big job ahead—stepping into the light, offering support, listening to women, and believing their stories.

"The world is finally listening," wrote Melinda Gates in *Time*. "2017 is proving to be a watershed moment for women in the workplace and beyond. Instead of being bullied into retreat or pressured into weary resignation, we are raising our voices—and raising them louder than ever before." When women feel that no one is listening, they stay silent and the toxic norms continue unchallenged. This is no longer as prevalent as it once was as women take collective action to protect each other from abuse and harassment.

"Despite substantial hurdles," Rudman and Glick wrote in *The Social Psychology of Gender*, "women have taken their place next to men in the workplace and are beginning to flex their muscle as powerful business and political leaders. As a result, although no one can guarantee that future progress will be smooth or linear, there is considerable cause for optimism that sexism in the workplace will continue to diminish over time."

While we may be flexing our muscles in politics and at work, we still have lots to do. It starts by making sure that our bosses, politicians, and contemporaries know that we have not granted men ownership of our bodies and our lives. That means we have not given them permission to harass us at work. It's disturbing to see how quickly even women's conversations about sexual misconduct veer into criticism of what she wore, what she said, where she went, and how much she drank. It was also sad to see women warriors who spoke up around the Grammys or the Olympic physician scandals being condemned and their activism discounted if they wore a low-cut gown or posed for a nude photo. By judging women in that way, we reinforce the idea that, regardless of a woman's thoughtful and courageous action, and no matter her organizing of other women for collective action, the truly important thing about her is the way she dresses. This judgment is ridiculous and demeaning and needs to stop.

BETTERBRAVE: RESOURCES FOR HARASSED WOMEN

Today, countless individual women are taking action to support each other and answer questions like, "How can the everyday worker, or the single mother holding down one or two minimum-wage jobs, fight back against abuse and harassment?" Tammy Cho and Grace

Choi are tackling that issue head on with BetterBrave. After the two women compared notes and shared their frustration, they were spurred into action and determined to do something. In an article for *Medium*, Choi wrote, "Tammy and I discussed this at length...we slowly opened up about our own experiences facing sexual harassment, discrimination, racism, and everything in between. It was a conversation that made us ask, 'Why don't good solutions to sexual harassment already exist?'"

The two women went on to talk to hundreds of people (including but not limited to targets of harassment, human resource departments, founders, investors, and employment lawyers) "to understand the full landscape of harassment." Then they worked with a friend and employment lawyer to translate their findings into guides for targets and for allies. As a result, BetterBrave provides resources, guides, tools, and employment lawyers to women who have been harassed.

Eliminating sexual harassment in the workplace is not only the right thing to do for a multitude of reasons, but it also makes good business sense. According to the EEOC's Select Task Force on the Study of Harassment in the Workplace, when employers consider the costs of workplace harassment, they often focus on legal costs, and with good reason. In 2015 the EEOC alone recovered $164.5 million for workers alleging harassment, and these direct costs are the least of it. The steepest cost is in the mental, physical, and economic harm to those who suffer it. Beyond that, workplace harassment affects all workers, and its true cost includes decreased productivity, increased turnover, and reputational harm. All of this drags down performance and the bottom line.

Speaking honestly about our experiences and supporting other women is the way to reveal the truth and insist on change. We can set the standards and—as the Amazonian shaman quoted in Chapter 1 said—women can make men stop. Imagine the benefits to our workplaces and communities when women, having gained equal power in work and life, finally eliminate sexual harassment and violence.

CHAPTER 9

CULTIVATING MEN AS ALLIES

“ We need to stop buying into the myth about gender equality. It isn't a reality yet.…[W]omen make up half of the US workforce, but the average working woman earns only 77 percent of what the average working man makes. But unless women and men both say this is unacceptable, things will not change.”

BEYONCÉ KNOWLES-CARTER, musician

While this is a book about ways women can help women improve their personal and professional success, let's keep in mind that men have an important role to play. This chapter focuses on how women can recruit men to the cause of equality and how they can talk with supportive men about these issues. This book is in no way an attack on men; we are truly "in this together," and we can't limit our support network exclusively to women. Gender equality is a big umbrella that includes men. Women who teach men how to step up as their allies win big at work and in life.

This is a perfect time to draw men in. Women are emboldened and inspired to ask for what they want and to support each other, and many men seem less inclined to actively oppose equality efforts than in the past. "Because changes toward equality continue to occur without the social world collapsing," Rudman and Glick pointed out in *The Social Psychology of Gender*, "men have become more likely to accept gender equality." This is great news, and it is also wonderful to hear that—although men still hold significantly more traditional attitudes about gender than women do—"data from the 1970s onward show that they also have become less sexist over time."

EQUALITY IS A WIN-WIN PROPOSITION

"What's in it for white men?" asked sociology professor Michael Kimmel in a video made by Elisa Kreisinger and available on *YouTube*. He said that all available evidence suggests that the more gender equality we can establish in our relationships, the better our health, the better our relationships with our spouses, the better our children do in school, the happier countries are, and the better corporations do. "This is a win-win all the way around," Kimmel said. "We have come to this idea that gender equality is a zero-sum game and if women win, men are going to lose. The reality is, when women win, men win as well."

Many men also perceive a bigger stake in women's equality today than in the past. They count on the financial contributions their wives make to the family economy, and they were likely raised by women who worked. Men who ignored their wives' complaints may respond to their daughters' outrage at encountering discrimination and barriers at work.

Equality Makes Everyone Happier

You might have heard recently about a few Nordic countries whose policies help their citizens score high on the happiness scale. They not only score higher than the US, but they score higher than other countries in Europe. The happiness scale grades countries on how evenly wealth is spread among the population, whether healthcare policies cover everyone, whether there is paid maternity and paternity leave, and how well women are represented in business and government. These are all factors that create more happiness through a higher quality of life for everyone.

Equality Benefits Men As Well As Women

Seeking fairness for everyone in the workplace includes developing family-friendly policies for *all* that do not penalize the childbearers, the childcarers, or the people who have no children. Many millennial men have said that they want to be hands-on fathers and have equal leave to do so. It's time to come together and work in common cause with men for gender-neutral policies that benefit everyone equally. We also need to insist from the start that dads take available paternity leave to do an equal share of childcare duties. Paternity leave helps establish equitable patterns right away, and these patterns tend to persist. Working for greater flexibility with policies in place is also important, as it lets people cover for each other and flex their work hours. Policies such as these allow new moms and dads the kind of flexibility that doesn't hinder their employers' productivity.

The data clearly show that gender equality, especially more women in leadership, is good for men too. It makes businesses more profitable, improving job security and prospects for everyone. More equality allows each person to contribute at the highest level, and feeling considered and appreciated improves employee satisfaction for everyone.

WHY WE NEED MEN AS ALLIES

Historically, any movement to advance women has been successful not in spite of men (okay, maybe in spite of *some* of them) but in partnership with them. So, we *know* how to work together. Men know this too. Countless men have told me that their mothers helped them become the good men they are today, and I'm sure their sisters, wives, and daughters continue to help them. In her book *ONE: How Male Allies Support Women for Gender Equality*, Julie Kratz highlighted the importance of identifying men who see inequality as a challenge to overcome and then working with those men to develop policies and practices that benefit everyone. This principle holds true in public life, private life, and the workplace.

It's important to find allies at every level in the company, including the upper levels of corporate management. "Men can take several powerful actions to help women's career development," said Deborah Gillis, former president and CEO of Catalyst. "The first is sponsorship—advocating for colleagues and putting their names forward for crucial assignments. While those in high-level positions have the most leverage to do that, sponsorship is something that anyone can do. It not only helps women colleagues have access to more opportunities, but sponsors also get recognized for identifying and nurturing top talent." Helping more women rise into leadership is an easy way to improve a company's prospects for success, so men—who make up the vast majority of well-positioned leaders—have a wonderful opportunity to help their firms succeed by sponsoring worthy women.

MEN WHO ARE NOT AWARE THERE IS A PROBLEM

Studies done by Catalyst, Fairygodboss, and others show that men's perspectives about equality in the workplace differ from women's. Women see the need for more women leaders, family-friendly schedules, and equal pay. Men, not so much. Men are not conscious of the discrepancy, so they don't even see it. It's almost as if women and men have been reading different books, isn't it? We all need to get on the same page together before we can write the next chapter. Don't assume that anyone, especially men, will understand what it's like to walk in your shoes unless you teach them what it's like to be a woman in your workplace.

Show Men the Problem: Call It Out

A lone man once attended a women's conference to find out how he could be a better ally for the women he worked with, said Emilie Aries, founder and CEO of Bossed Up. Seeing the issues through his eyes led her to realize how many men don't get that perspective unless it's shown to them explicitly.

An effective way to get men to recognize the disparities and issues that women face is to get them to "read the comments section of a woman's article on the Internet," wrote Lambda Legal's Anne Krook. "Read what male readers say in the comments section about women's articles: pay particular [attention] to comments on articles about science, technology, or sports." Just like we ask people to believe women who talk about harassment, "you should also believe the men mean what they say if they call women cunts and hope they are raped. To feel the weight of the comments, read them out loud, and imagine them directed to your mother, sister, wife, daughter, or any woman you love and respect."

> Don't assume that anyone, especially men, will understand what it's like to walk in your shoes unless you teach them what it's like to be a woman in your workplace.

GETTING MEN TO SUPPORT WOMEN

With so few women in the C-suite and upper management, many women say their best mentors and allies have been men. Executive recruiter Summer Anderson said she met her first mentor at twenty-five years old when she tried to sell him life insurance. He told her that he admired her perseverance and ability to cold call and that he would like to hire her. Three years later he did, and she learned executive search from the ground up. She had role models and women she admired from afar, but in her industry most of her allies and sponsors were men.

Who are the men in your workplace who meet the criteria for allies? Look for a man who:

- Can turn his good intentions into lasting change if women will tell him truthfully and openly the ways gender inequality has affected them

- Has shown through his words and actions that he is committed to gender equality
- Is willing to have the difficult conversations on your behalf when you're not in the room
- Is willing to mentor and sponsor women to create opportunities for female leadership within your company

Even if you have encountered some angry white men at work, don't abandon your search for allies.

Of course, white men are angry at losing their privileges. "So I say welcome white men. You've officially joined the Fu**ed Over Club," said Elisa Kreisinger in her video "What's the Deal with White Men?" on *YouTube*. Women didn't cause men's loss of security, prestige, or the ability to earn enough to support a full-time wife at home, pay the mortgage on a home to raise their kids, or retire comfortably on a single income, she said, although women can understand why men would find their loss of privilege painful. "Does this mean we let white male fragility and anger hold us hostage?" Kreisinger asked. "Nope. We continue to challenge men on their behavior, support masculinity that doesn't benefit from putting others down, and encourage men to support each other."

HOW TO COMMUNICATE WITH MALE ALLIES

In her book *ONE*, Kratz listed ten common ways that allies can support their female colleagues and concluded the list with this observation: "When we assembled these top ten support mechanisms, we were astounded by the common denominator—communication."

In fact, the common thread in all efforts to involve men in eliminating gender inequality, from involvement in historical women's struggles, like suffrage, to making themselves vulnerable by sticking their necks out to support women at work today, is one single strategy: communication.

Catalyst reported that men's support for gender equality can be engaged by appealing to their sense of fairness. In addition, shifting away from a win-or-lose mentality to recognizing that everyone benefits from gender equality can lead men to become greater advocates who endorse our efforts to change unfair practices.

There are many things we can do together:

- We can commit ourselves to voicing our values and concerns when we see those values being violated.
- We can identify internal issues and challenge policies that inhibit women from rising into leadership.
- We can speak openly about the benefits of equality and how they contribute to the overall success of the company.
- We can talk about how to achieve mutually beneficial goals.

Communicate with your ally about your needs and goals and discuss biases, assumptions, and oppressive patterns of behavior that you observe at work. Think together strategically about how to address any issues that are inhibiting your ability to do your work, achieve your goals, and thrive in your relationships with your coworkers. Ultimately, open communication about these issues lets women and their allies develop positive working relationships based on their shared values. Communication will also create opportunities for collaboration among peers. From the outset women and their allies can agree to work together, share in the rewards of success, and give credit where credit is due.

Reassure your ally that you are neither holding him responsible nor expecting him to solve women's problems; you only want him to become more aware. "Simply acknowledging someone's challenge—not necessarily solving it—can have a huge impact on how they're doing and how included they feel at work," said Aubrey Blanche, global head of diversity and inclusion at Atlassian. She described the impact of Australia's divisive 2017 marriage equality survey on the company's LGBTQ+ employees. "We decided to show support the best way we knew how: By lighting up our Sydney HQ in rainbow lights, printing 'love is love' T-shirts, and acknowledging it at our companywide town hall meetings," Blanche said. "Hearing my colleagues say they felt recognized and safe because of these small actions [has] fundamentally changed my view: I can be a better teammate just by providing empathy—not just solutions."

THE POTENTIAL IMPACT OF MILLENNIALS

One bright spot as we make progress toward gender equality at work: there are reasons to believe that millennial men will be great allies. Demographics reveal that by the year 2020 millennials will make up half of the global workforce, according to an infographic in "Revealing the Real Millennials" by Catalyst, and it's widely believed that millennials, including the men, expect a work-life balance that allows them to participate more equally in their families.

"Broadly speaking, millennial men and women share similar values about gender and LGBTQ+ rights," said Sarah Acer, herself a millennial and creative agency founder, in a telephone conversation with my producer. "By 2020, this generation will be the majority of the workforce and they are moving into real positions of power. They view diversity as a positive and millennial men are less concerned about their supervisor's gender than in their leadership abilities. Millennials want measurable results and to see systemic problems solved in their lifetime. They are fed up that people in power aren't doing anything about it." Acer said she is encouraged to see this educated populace is conscious and demanding change.

When allies can join their agendas and bring people together, they will make collective action more effective.

Millennials' well-defined expectations could provide a seismic shift when it comes to gender equality in the workplace. Tina Tchen, the lawyer spearheading the TIME'S UP legal defense fund, is impressed with the approach that millennials are taking. "What strikes me as different about the next generation is how they're translating their personal lives into their activism," said Tchen in a *HuffPost* interview with Kelley Calkins. "They're really putting themselves out there in a way I don't think my generation did." When allies can join their agendas and bring people together, they will make collective action more effective.

Teach Millennial Men to See

The strengths of millennials go beyond the expectations they bring to the workplace; their more egalitarian attitudes should also help reduce the discriminatory practices that have hurt women in previous generations. Mindset alone isn't going to be enough to turn the tide, however, and a 2015 Catalyst poll, discussed in the report "Revealing the Real Millennials," found that there are still some striking differences in attitudes between millennial men and women. While currently the majority of millennial men think their employers are promoting gender diversity through training, open communication, and publicizing gender diversity principles, 90 percent of millennial women feel that gender discrimination is still an issue in the workplace, and 84 percent of women agree that there are inherent workplace biases that hold women back and that a significant pay gap exists. These differences in perception point to a communication challenge for women in their pursuit of equality. No one wants to see himself as part of a group that is holding others back, but our inability to feel another person's disadvantage does not make that person's struggle any less painful. Women can teach them to see.

Young Men Can Help Break the Glass Ceiling

Openness to education is a great step forward. Millennial men "are willing to change their behaviors to support greater gender diversity," according to a report from the Boston Consulting Group (BCG) written by Katie Abouzahr and her colleagues. "Companies should engage them in shaping family policies and supporting women's issues....Companies that engage young men in helping to break the glass ceiling will not only build a stronger culture and improve their operational and financial performance, they will also differentiate themselves in the recruiting marketplace and develop a richer pipeline of talent." Programs that empower and elevate women leaders are great, but companies that are genuinely committed to gender equality will recruit and invest in like-minded young men as well.

HOW ALLIES CAN HELP

Asking men to help can create significant gains. In 2017 BCG released a sweeping workplace gender diversity study, "Getting the Most from Your Diversity Dollars," that involved more than 17,500 participants in twenty-one countries. Exhibit 5 in the report indicates that 96 percent of respondents reported progress in companies where men were actively involved in gender diversity, compared to only 30 percent at companies where men didn't actively promote diversity. That's a huge difference!

Women are often reluctant to ask men to become allies because they do not expect the men they work with to help them. This is a mistake. To be sure, there's no point in trying to persuade the office misogynist to help women advance, but when you identify men who are open to learning, you can help educate them. Men can be great allies, and they play a key role in preventing, highlighting, and reporting situations where harassment occurs. Create a call to action for them to improve their company by advancing women, and highlight stories of men's successes working for equality and safety for women. Ask around in your community and industry to find out about the good guys. Amplify this by praising their example at work, in company newsletters or blogs, and encourage your local business journal to start a feature.

Men can be great allies, and they play a key role in preventing, highlighting, and reporting situations where harassment occurs.

Transformational leadership coach Regina Huber recently told me of a recurring theme in conversations she's had with men who support gender equality. "I hear from men, 'I'd like to help, but I really don't know what to do.' So, we have to ask them."

1. **Support flexible work policies that benefit men as well as women, such as part-time employment, remote work, and parental leave.** Getting men involved removes the stigma from these flexibility policies that help long-term career development for women. "The best way for men to challenge stereotypes and support workplace flexibility is by actually taking advantage of these policies themselves," noted the writers at Fairygodboss. "The more men who do this at the senior level, especially, the more empowered all employees will feel to follow their example."

2. **Model the right behaviors to make sure everyone is treated fairly and analyze whether or not policies consider the needs of everyone who works there.** "Are all people being paid the same and getting the same opportunities for promotions, travel, or special development?" asked BCG partner Ant Roediger. Once you have the data, convene a diverse group to decide how to correct any inequities. It's also a good idea to get involved with company-specific initiatives. "Diversity programs become much more effective when both men and women are part of them, and having men be co-sponsors goes a long way," BCG partner and managing director Michael Tan said. Equality benefits everyone, and it requires support from everyone before it will become reality.

3. **Communicate fairly with all genders, and make sure all coworkers get an equal turn to speak and that performance evaluations for everyone focus on actions, not personalities.** "Part of being an ally is about being a sounding board for decisions people need to make about their career and about issues they're facing in their work," said Roediger. "I try to reach out formally and informally to offer that."

4. **Sponsor high-potential women.** "Sponsorship is advocating for someone; it's when you're sitting in a meeting and people are discussing promotions and you stick your neck out to say, 'I think this person would be great,'" explained Abouzahr in the Fairygodboss article. "It's more than mentorship. It's taking accountability to advocate for someone." Sponsorship is critical for women in middle management and above, because the path to advancement may be less clear and a more senior manager can point the way forward.

CELEBRATE YOUR ALLIES

Today, women are leading the charge in the fight for equality at work, but we will not achieve parity without the support of men. Disparity is the result of exclusion. Parity will be the result of inclusion as women and men discover what they have in common, establish real and fair outcomes, and work side by side to accomplish their goals.

"I believe it's important to talk about the men who are champions for diversity, inclusion and supporting women to succeed," said Michelle Peluso, CMO of IBM. "If we tell the stories of these men, it will help other men have examples to emulate....The battle for equality is one of culture, and it will only be won if men feel just as compelled as we do to make the future better."

Parity is an ideal that I hope to see become a reality in my lifetime. It will happen through the efforts of those who stand together to create a better, more equitable way forward for everyone. People of all genders have always allied with each other to raise families, build communities, run businesses, and more. We have an equal stake in raising girls and women to equal status, and we can and will do this together.

CHAPTER 10
WHAT YOU CAN SAY AND DO

ff An enemy is one whose story we have not heard. **JJ**

GENE KNUDSEN HOFFMAN, compassionate listening pioneer

Relationships across genders are complicated, and most of us have built up a lot of clutter over a lifetime. Part 3 exemplifies our ambivalent interdependence, since we began by talking about sexual harassment and violence and ended talking about recruiting men as allies. Whatever ideas we may have developed about people in the past, we need to find clear, respectful, and positive ways to communicate and create relationships with everyone at work.

In 2017 women's collective action and use of social media finally drew public attention to the disaster of sexual assault for women from many industries. These actions seem to have also ended job security for men who previously felt safe behaving as sexual predators, harassers, or bullies. A few high-profile abusers have lost their jobs, and many men are now nervous about what to say to women. This is a great start, and we need to keep the spotlight on, keep listening to and believing women, and keep inviting men to help stop harassment and violence in the workplace.

ESTABLISH YOUR LEADERSHIP

Fortunately, women are being heard as never before, and our support can help increase the safety and success of the many women who are still abused, including women of color and those who work in low-status jobs or fields heavily dominated by men. People who abuse their powerful positions to dominate, bully, demean, attack, or obtain sexual gratification need to be fired and possibly tried for crimes. The small percentage of men who rape and assault women coworkers will continue to do so until their organizations make them stop or fire them—action that has to start at the top and work its way down.

This is not a declaration of war or an attack on all men, but it is a refusal to allow men to continue to harm women. All people need to come together at work, talk openly about these issues, keep working for progress, and stop these criminals.

First of all, please trust your instincts if you feel that things are not right. There is nothing wrong with you. You are not imagining these workplace problems, although some people would like you to think so. The scenarios and scripts in this chapter can be modified to fit a wide variety of situations. With support from other women, we are overcoming the self-doubt that has kept us from stepping forward with confidence. By calmly standing up for what you believe and saying that women deserve equal treatment and protection at work, you can establish yourself as a leader.

Gather Support at Work

Your chances of making change are better if you have a connected group, so get to know your coworkers and create a safe opportunity for people to talk about feeling vulnerable. Nearly everyone has felt different or excluded at some time. Acknowledge that you have heard them and ask what would have made the situation better for them. Telling your own story will encourage others to make their voices heard. Linda Seabrook, general counsel for Futures Without Violence, said leaders will ask two important questions about the status of women in the company:

1. How many women are in leadership positions at the company?
2. Are women heard?

The answers to these two questions will reveal a great deal about the company's attitudes and approach. Present facts from this book about the benefits of women leaders when you make your case for hiring and promoting more women. See Chapter 4 for ways to learn about pay scales.

By calmly standing up for what you believe and saying that women deserve equal treatment and protection at work, you can establish yourself as a leader.

AMPLIFY THROUGH THE MEDIA

Abusers need to be outed to be stopped, and the media has been called the Third Witness. No voice is louder than theirs. Attorney Gloria Allred used the media effectively in her work to stop sexual predators. For example, the secret *Facebook* group Marines United, which had 30,000 members, routinely posted nude pictures of female Marines online, said Allred. The men openly described the violent sexual assaults they wanted to perform on them, and Allred alleged the Marine Corps entirely ignored this behavior.

In a 2017 *Task & Purpose* article called "The Rise and Fall (and Rise) of 'Marines United,'" senior editor Jared Keller detailed a long and convoluted history of misogyny against women in the Marine Corps. Although *Facebook* reportedly shut down Marines United quickly in response to complaints of nudity in 2016, Marines United 2.0 and two different Marines United 3.0 groups quickly popped up, Keller wrote. Likening the effort to a game of Whac-A-Mole, Keller noted, "The Marines have the smallest proportion of women in its ranks, as well as the highest rate of sexual assault compared to other branches." He went on to conclude, "In the eyes of vets and active-duty service members interviewed by *Task & Purpose*, the Corps has been heading for a come-to-Jesus moment for years."

Allred's publicity efforts helped encourage the US House of Representatives to unanimously pass a bill proposed by Republican representative Martha McSally from Arizona to make nonconsensual sharing of intimate photographs a violation of the Uniform Code of Military Justice. Provisions of the bill were incorporated into the National Defense Authorization Act for 2018 and signed by the president at the end of 2017.

Allred called what she does "creative lawyering." Because sexual harassment, assault, and rape come down to her word against his, she amplifies a victim's story in "the court of public opinion by getting the victim's perspective in the news" through well-timed and orchestrated press conferences. Allred, who represents roughly half of Bill Cosby's nearly sixty accusers, stated that if perpetrators know there are consequences, it will stop some of them. Cosby was convicted in April 2018 of three counts of sexual assault.

SPEAK UP TO CHALLENGE DISRESPECT

Sidelining, isolating, intimidating, and speaking over women are the normalizing behaviors at the bottom of the abuse pyramid that invite sexual harassment and violence in the workplace. Work to cultivate a culture of support and respect by speaking out and standing up for others. Never allow a sexist remark to go unchallenged, but instead ask:

- "What did you mean by that?"
- "What were you trying to say?"

TEACH MEN HOW TO TREAT WOMEN

As we said in Chapter 8, the vast majority of harassment situations at work are not criminal assaults, although they annoy, demean, and enrage women. Men often feel entitled to say whatever they want to a woman, and our society teaches boys that a girl's "no" might actually mean "maybe." That doesn't mean you have to give them a pass, though. No passes here! Instead, you have the right and responsibility to define the boundaries of what you will tolerate. Your goal is to keep communication on a professional level. In Chapter 7 we talked about using strategic communication. Practice that at every level and in every situation and consider the consequences of what you say.

Communication Sandwiches

It is hard for anyone to deliver an unwelcome message, and what I call the Updated Sandwich is a technique that can help. Start with a slice of genuine appreciation for the other person that's related in some way to your concern. Add a digestible portion of filling (your specific complaint, correction, or request). Top with another slice of genuine appreciation or praise. It sounds like this:

Slice: *Kevin, I appreciate the way you contribute helpful ideas to our group discussions.*

Filling: *What would help you notice that you often interrupt Iesha, so you can stop doing it? It's rude, it annoys her, and it keeps her from sharing her good ideas.*

Slice: *You are an excellent team player, Kevin, and I'm counting on your teamwork to help everyone contribute at their highest level.*

Arm Ourselves for Safety

"Now, all at once, women are refusing to accept sexual aggression as any kind of award, and men are getting fired from their jobs," wrote novelist Barbara Kingsolver. "It feels like an earthquake…. We've spent so much life-force on looking good but not too good, being professional but not unapproachable, while the guys just got on with life. And what of the massive costs of permanent vigilance, the tense smiles, declined work assignments and lost chances that are our daily job of trying to avoid assault?" She sat with her daughters while each practiced saying powerful phrases, until they could speak firmly and emphatically without their voices shaking:

Don't say that to me. Don't do that to me. I hate it.

Don't laugh uncomfortably. Don't try to soften it. Say it like you mean it.

Create Workplace Programs That Can Help

If several people at work are struggling with harassment issues, strategize with other women to propose that the company begin to track issues related to harassment, leadership, communication, and pay. For example, keep records of complaints and how they are resolved, audit the gender and ethnic composition of the leadership team, communicate openly about efforts and progress, and become transparent about pay rates for comparable jobs. Employees need a system through which they can readily provide both qualitative and quantitative feedback about issues of harassment and inequality. This will help create a culture of sharing and transparency, instead of one of shaming and toxic masculinity.

Protecting anonymity is very important, so an excellent way to gather information is through an anonymous survey so employees feel safe answering honestly. Then report the results company-wide and ask for suggestions about a workplace strategy.

CLUELESS COWORKER

There's a big difference between awkward adolescent stupidity and malicious predatory behavior, and it shouldn't be hard to distinguish between the two. People in the first category don't intend harm. They don't know what to say or how to act and are basically clueless. I think many men find women mysterious and lack confidence in their ability to predict how women will respond to them. Many people are insensitive to their effect on others, but they may also be willing to be educated in a friendly and nonjudgmental manner. Such education will be more effective if several women plan together and consistently deliver the same messages to the clueless ones. Say a coworker regularly makes inappropriate comments to you, which makes you uncomfortable. The best way for a coworker to understand what he's doing wrong is for you to be honest and tell him what you think and want. If possible, it's always best to give him the benefit of the doubt while probing for more information:

- "Gosh, what you just said hurt my feelings. Was that your intention?"
- "Wow, did you really mean what you just said about women? Is that what you meant to say to me?"
- "I don't want to hurt your feelings and I want to understand you. What made you say that?"
- "What are you trying to accomplish by saying or doing that?"
- "That's not okay! Perhaps you didn't mean to offend me, but please stop."
- "It may be that you were just joking, but please don't say that. It's making me uncomfortable."
- "What do you want me to say to that?"
- "Excuse me?"
- "Would you repeat that?"
- "Ouch!"
- "I want to have a solid professional relationship with you. Let's agree on the best ways to talk together so we don't offend each other."
- "Are you willing to hear how your comments make me feel? If we understand each other better, we can work together more effectively."
- "I need your help to establish some ground rules in our working relationship. What would you suggest?" [Listen] "Okay, here are some other ideas I had."

Imagine that you are an anthropologist trying to understand an unfamiliar custom that mystifies you (you are, kind of). You are not taking offense; you are just trying to make sense of it without giving offense yourself. Another approach is to repeat back in a neutral tone what you heard the other person say. Mirroring his comments like this can help him to feel heard, and if it's not what he meant, you can work out the differences together. Often conflict arises from simple misunderstandings.

HOSTILE COWORKER WITH BIAS

If your friendly efforts to establish boundaries and a good working relationship are rebuffed, you may be dealing with a coworker who is actively hostile. "Never respond in kind. If you are a recipient of an email, memo, text or post that lashes out and is negative, personal, discriminatory and accusatory, resist the urge to respond with emotion," suggested Michele Weldon in "Google This: Best Ways to Handle a Hostile Coworker Who Shows Gender Bias" on TaketheLeadWomen.com. Report this to your supervisor and don't gossip about it with your coworkers. "You do not want this to escalate. Know that communicating in a way that can be considered harassment is illegal," Weldon wrote. Document the offensive language and actions, and store copies of emails, tweets, or images on a home computer.

As soon as possible after the harassment event, work with other women to organize a discussion around solutions for gender bias and discrimination, Weldon wrote. Don't focus on a specific event, but talk about creating a healthy environment where all employees can contribute their best. Pull together a panel with a facilitator, experts, or even respected coworkers. A reading list could help everyone understand the terms. Weldon quoted Gloria Feldt, who teaches, "Moments of controversy are the best times to make progress because people are paying attention." Don't let the discussion become accusatory or a gripe session, but do have the group develop action steps for improvement.

HAVE CONVERSATIONS THAT MATTER

No one can sit on the sidelines as long as there are victims suffering in our workplaces. If your management won't get involved, you can still be proactive. Jennifer Siebel Newsom of The Representation Project suggested that we have conversations about what it means to "be a man" and to talk about consent and respecting each other's boundaries. It's also possible that a woman might harass men she works with and then cry foul, so men need chances to speak their truth too. Looking the other way lets sexual predators get away with it. You could also watch Newsom's film *The Mask You Live In* to learn more about the causes and consequences of toxic masculinity.

> Looking the other way lets sexual predators get away with it.

Remember that we all have biases, many of which we acquired decades ago and which are affected by how and where we grew up. Discussing your differences with others is a great conversation to have, and you may be surprised when you see the situation from another person's point of view. Listen, learn, and ask respectfully for what you want.

THE IMPORTANCE OF LISTENING

One of the biggest frustrations in the workplace is feeling that we are not being heard. It is a rare and beautiful thing when a person truly believes and knows others are listening. Listen, and repeat back to be clear you heard correctly: *You said...* In a recent post on listening, international fundraiser Kathy LeMay wrote about being silent for an entire year while listening to her donors. She learned that everyone feels overwhelmed. As she listened, people expressed feelings, shared their problems, and began to look for ways to help. When she stopped talking, she was able to better understand their motivations, and they began to view her as a trusted colleague.

Deep Listening

Anyone can learn to become a better listener. Gene Knudsen Hoffman, a compassionate listening pioneer, brought the art of listening from the Quaker meetinghouse onto the world stage and became a legend in peacemaking circles, including the workplace.

Continuing the work Hoffman started, Dennis Rivers wrote a workbook to help us understand each other and reach agreement in daily life. "Listen first and acknowledge what you hear, even if you don't agree with it, before expressing your experience or point of view," Rivers wrote. To do this, make a brief summary, repeating what you think you heard and acknowledging the speaker's point of view. This kind of listening "separates acknowledging from approving or agreeing," Rivers said.

- "Mark, you are sending me to meet Mr. Elsworth for dinner on Friday night. Who else will be there? And what do you want me to accomplish with that meeting?"
- "Bob, are you appointing me to serve on a committee with six men to recruit more women into the new department? What is my role and what are your goals for it?"

Expressing your concerns is acceptable as long as you allow the speaker to address the possible outcomes that might worry you or to modify the request.

- "I understand that you have a huge crush on Lydia, but Jeffrey, it's not appropriate for me to ask her to go out with you. It could harm my ability to work with both of you."

ADAPT COMMUNICATION STYLE

In addition to becoming great listeners, women need to practice the art of the brief response in order to keep men's attention. Women tend to build relationships with their communication and go into detail and backstories to present their case. Men tend to want results from their communication and mostly want to get to the point, whether they are discussing sports or their recent promotion.

My coauthor Dr. Lois Frankel urged women to "get to the point" in *Leading Women*. She said that women mistakenly believe that saying more words will increase their authority. The opposite is true. Frankel said, "Fewer words strengthen a message, but more words soften it." Say the most important thing first, and then substantiate it with a few important points only if he asks for more information.

> *Karen:* Mr. Brown, we need to update our company harassment policy.
> *Mr. Brown:* Why?
> *Karen:* It leaves the company vulnerable to expensive legal action.
> *Mr. Brown:* What's the fix?
> *Karen:* A team can update it to protect our company and employees.
> *Mr. Brown:* What would that involve?
> *Karen:* Joe, Susie, and I are willing to find examples from other companies and make some recommendations for you to review in about four weeks.

You don't mention your frustrations with the existing policy or his wimpy response to complaints. He doesn't need to know you have worked for six months to find a team willing to tackle this. You state the facts and ask for what you want. Boil down your communication to the most important points and stick to it. Practice, and if necessary, get a partner to help you present your case. Make your point, ask for what you want, say thanks, and move on.

One Is Plenty

My *Leading Women* coauthor Claire Damken Brown shared a one-is-enough strategy that helps women keep men's attention. "Think: 'one is plenty.' Answer with one word: yes, no, or maybe. If he needs more information, he will ask."

For example, a man asks, "Will you talk with the customer on Thursday?"

She says, "No." (One word)

He asks, "When will you talk with that customer?"

She replies, "Probably early Friday, if I get all the data on time from Bob." (One sentence)

Wanting more information, he asks, "Are there issues with Bob's work that I should know about?"

She states, "Bob has been sick and out of the office for a few days. He has the data and I was not able to contact him. He's back now and we've talked a few times. He'll get his data to me Thursday and I will add it to the report and talk with the customer Friday. I will set up a conference call today for Friday morning." (One paragraph)

MANAGING INTERRUPTIONS

Being talked over is another way women feel disadvantaged and disrespected at work, and Claire Damken Brown offered these phrases for managing interruptions: "'Just a second,' 'I'm not quite done yet,' 'I'll be with you in a moment,' 'One minute while I finish,' 'Thanks for that insight, I'll finish now,' 'I'll continue now without interruptions,' or "Hold that thought.'" A woman can directly look at the interrupter, establish momentary eye contact, and "make a statement, using the person's name if she knows it: 'Bryan, I'll take comments in a moment.' She then continues talking to the group and completes her ideas. She may reestablish her dominance as speaker by leaning forward in the direction of the interrupter, speaking louder, and if seated, standing up to draw attention back to her."

CHANGE THE CULTURE

If you are interested in changing the culture, analyze the power structure to gain a realistic idea of the support for change. Who is in charge and what are their priorities? What is your relationship with them? Is there anyone interested in building the business who doesn't have gender bias? Be daring, yet honest with yourself.

Your goal is company policies that produce fair *practices* for all employees. The first step is to rally support among your coworkers so you can approach management with a united front. Next, connect with coworkers who are willing to read and help formulate policies and procedures. Admittedly, this is not for everyone. If the company already has a policy and procedure for dealing with harassment that is not effective or is not enforced, you can offer to chair or serve on a committee to assess the need and address the issue.

Make certain that you don't make it women against men, cautioned Feldt. Avoid this mistake by including men in conversations about bias and getting them on the committee. Diverse and inclusive companies are more profitable, and everyone has a stake in that. You are doing a service to the company, preventing a potentially out-of-control issue in your workplace.

WRITE IT DOWN

I learned in forensics training, "If it's not written down, it does not exist." Policies should address sexual and domestic violence and sexual harassment and should provide for regular review. Every company needs clear policies that address respectful discourse and disagreement and set out real penalties for offensive behavior, Feldt noted. A little online research will provide models for supporting diversity and inclusion. The interests of the committee members will dictate the specifics, and everything from hiring practice to gender-neutral bathrooms could be on the table.

Work to ensure that the performance review process requires supervisors to acknowledge and penalize employees for abusive behavior reported at work, and that the complaint procedure guarantees confidentiality. Employee participation in training programs should be required and go beyond one-time sessions. Engage everyone in the workplace with bystander intervention training.

When building the business case for changes, make sure to ground your proposals in facts, Weldon wrote. Everyone has opinions they consider to be facts, but make sure to gather actual current evidence, studies, and research about the most productive and inclusive workplaces. If someone offers an unsupported claim, Weldon suggested you reply kindly, "That's interesting. The most recent research has debunked that theory, though. I am happy to send it to you."

Filmmaker Newsom agreed that it's important to fight backlash. "If you hear someone talking about how it's 'dangerous' to be a man right now—remind them that the facts don't support that argument. The victims of this epidemic are NOT the men who face consequences. The victims are the victims, end of story."

ASK QUESTIONS AND LISTEN

Women know we can't do this alone. To adopt a new process, build a business, end abuses, or help women advance, we need to gather allies who want the best for the company. Ask men to talk about the ally issue from a man's point of view. Ask questions to find out what his concerns are for the company and speak to those.

Share the data showing the benefits of a more diverse workforce for a company like yours. Practice with other women before you talk with your ally about improving the company culture and where your company stands in the parity ratio.

- "This report shows that profits go up 18 percent when women and men develop strategies together. How can we use this information to boost our performance?"
- "Do you have five minutes to give me feedback on an idea I have for protecting the company from liability?" [Sketch out your plan to strengthen the harassment policy.]
- "May I show you something that's interfering with our ability to recruit and retain good women? I'd like to hear your thoughts." [Show the year-end figures on pay gap between men and women.]

> **"** Personally, I haven't encountered major challenges related to my sex because I have always been able to enlist male advocates on my side. At the United Nations, in my business, and in my community activities, I have always found a way to collaborate with men.**"**
>
> JANET C. SALAZAR,
> cofounder and CEO of
> IMPACT Leadership 21

Talk privately and invite him to notice when women are ignored or talked over, something men often do not perceive. Then suggest ways that he could speak up in different situations and use his privilege to help women get equal time at the table.

- "We've heard from everyone here except Patricia. Do you have anything to add?"
- "Wait a minute, Rob. Isn't that the idea Courtney expressed a few minutes ago? Let's make sure we understand it before we elaborate on her plan."
- "That's a great proposal, Brooke. Can you and Dan work that up for the meeting next week?"

Work to turn a mentor into a sponsor by developing a solid, trusting, professional, and two-way relationship. Find ways that you can help the sponsor in return: research, focus groups, assistance with his challenges, admiration, appreciation, positive public relations, etc. When an opportunity you want to pursue comes up, ask him to advocate for you when you are not in the room.

Please tell them I would be a good fit for that management job. These are my relevant credentials, and these past experiences prove I'm comfortable with the risks and pressures it would involve.

PRAISE THE GUYS WHO GET IT

Men sometimes feel beleaguered and worry that they can't say or do anything right. Recognizing men for their mentorship, sponsorship, and promotion of women into senior positions is very important, Julie Kratz noted, and it provides an opportunity to inform everyone in the company about the value women bring to the organization. Make sure they know why it's a good idea to hire, promote, and pay women what they deserve.

I hear you helped Sonia get that sales directorship. She is fantastic and has ideas that will really boost our sales. That was a very smart move. Thank you for promoting worthy women.

Give the Good Guys Awards

Rayona Sharpnack, an expert in gender issues and women's leadership, took the recognition idea several steps farther by creating an awards program. She wanted to recognize and praise men "for hiring the best people for the job—who often happen to be women—treating them fairly and paying them equally," according to the Guys Who Get It Awards website. Awards like this call attention to the ways that gender balance improves a company's profits, innovation, customer satisfaction, and employee engagement. Although some have complained that men should not get awards for simply doing the right, smart thing, Sharpnack said in an email that this acclaim provides role models for the guys who think they get it but still have a lot to learn. It also shifts women's attention to finding and partnering with allies who can help us reach parity.

Think about your opportunities to incorporate praise and appreciation for allies. I once attended a Diversity Woman conference where Dr. Sheila Robinson proudly introduced the "Male Advocates," who stood to resounding applause. Several corporate CEOs spoke of the importance of diversity and women leaders and the support men should give them.

GET MEN TO ADVOCATE

Everyone benefits from diverse ideas in the workplace. Study after study has found increased profitability of companies with more women in leadership and more diverse teams, although some executives don't yet know this. Don't miss this educational opportunity.

If you don't have direct access to people in the C-suite, make an ally of someone who does by getting to know them. Administrative assistants, often women, control access to execs and may help bring pertinent information to their bosses' attention. The Selected Bibliography at the back of this book lists articles on the many benefits in profitability, recruitment, and retention that women leaders deliver to companies. Find one that resonates for your industry, print it, and show it to your boss. Share information about ways that a competitor has advanced through the actions of a woman leader. Point out new promotions of women to C-Suites in your industry.

Encourage the men you work with to stop and listen deeply to what women are saying about the issues, and to never assume they know her experience, and praise them for doing so. Urge them not to "mansplain" by telling women what they ought to do to solve "their problem." Make clear that you don't expect your ally to fix it, but to offer his perspective so you can work together on a solution. Here are some things you could suggest they say:

- Ally: "Please tell me your experience with gender bias and how it has affected your career."
- Ally: "What kind of sexual harassment have you experienced? What can we do to keep that from happening here?"
- Ally: "Is there anything in our facility or system that's making it difficult for you to do your job?"

Create opportunities for men and women of various ages and life stages so they can learn from other points of view. As they develop rapport, men can help women advocate for themselves and work together to amplify their voices. Especially, ask men to press their peers to treat all women better, and not to allow sexist views to undermine women's credibility.

Shine Your Light

If you have a hard time speaking up in a group, join Toastmasters or another speaking club, or get a relationship with a coach. Tabby Biddle helps women find the courage to stand up, tell their stories, and speak their truth, including preparing TED Talks. Only 17 percent of TED speakers are women, not because TED doesn't accept them, but because women don't apply. Whether in meetings, on blogs, or in letters to the editor (yes, people still read newspapers), submit your ideas and speak out. Toot your horn; tell your story. Let's work to build on our accomplishments, concentrate on our abundant talents, and reach parity together.

We really are "in this together," so every person has a role in elevating women at work. Anne Krook, chair of the board of directors of Lambda Legal, has decades of experience in tech industries dominated by men. She said we need to acknowledge women's contributions and expertise, ask that more women be included, contradict demeaning statements, and correct sexist remarks.

- "Thanks so much for helping with [complicated thing]; that was great." Say it out loud and by email and copy others.
- "Another really valuable part of Julie's idea is the money it will make for us."
- "Let's ask Colleen about that; she was so smart about the last problem we had with that."
- "Can we add Roxanne? She has so much expertise in that area." This is stronger than "Why aren't there women on this panel?"
- Counter dismissive statements with "Actually, she's really smart. I always ask her first about [topic]. She killed it on [project]."
- "Don't call [named woman colleague] a bitch."

It's particularly important for relatively senior men to call out other relatively senior men in front of junior men, Krook noted. By standing up for and supporting one another, we can create and leave a legacy of gender equality for all employees.

On a Roll

Women today are no longer afraid to boldly support the person who is the best candidate for the job, regardless of gender, and to condemn the harassing words and violent behaviors that have ruined so many women's lives and careers. Let's work together with other women and men to use our many strengths to create a better world for all.

CHAPTER 11
LET'S DO THIS

❝First we wanted men to do something for us. But that time is gone now. We're not going to ask men to change the world. We're going to do it ourselves.❞

MALALA YOUSAFZAI, Nobel Peace Prize recipient

I hear a news item nearly every day that shows what women can do when they listen to each other, believe each other, and support each other. Everywhere, women are supporting change, expanding the arenas in which they act, and using their strength and power to advance toward equality.

Despite our progress, it's easy to see how many challenges women still face, one of which is not to become depressed and demoralized by those very challenges! So here's where I focus when I start to feel discouraged: I know that life is beautiful, that we are put on this earth to experience love and joy, and that most people are good and want to help each other. I choose to surround myself with people like that, and to have all the fun I can while trying to do good.

We've offered a lot of ideas in this book, and I hope you do not feel overwhelmed by so many options. No one can do everything, but each of us can do something. Why not start with one idea? One woman. One helpful act. One request to connect. One. And tomorrow—another one. I know that when you get this energy going in your life, it will grow and change you in ways that will amaze you.

LIVING THROUGH A WATERSHED MOMENT

"By any measure, 2017 was a turning point," wrote Gloria Feldt in *Time*. "It started with the largest collective global protest march, when women in pink hats and the best activist signs ever showed up, woke up and made clear that something fundamental was changing." Powerful men toppled; women funded the #TimesUp initiative to offer support; and Oprah's speech at the Golden Globes, where the majority of women wore black in solidarity with one another, galvanized audiences.

On another front, Olympic physician Larry Nassar at last began serving a prison sentence after abusing Olympic athletes for decades. Individual women have long spoken out and been ignored, but this movement has been different. So what happened to create this watershed moment? "Women and girls banded together to fight for themselves because no one else would do it," said Rachael Denhollander, who first made Nassar's abuse public in 2016. Denhollander nailed it: what's different now is that women realize that their power lies in acting together and they have joined forces.

Entertainment and athletics are just two market sectors working to get ahead of the tsunami of women's outrage, and other businesses will follow suit. "To stay ahead of the curve in the marketplace and attract top candidates," continued Feldt, "businesses will need to advance gender parity in the workplace."

We will keep the momentum for change going by gathering our allies, making the business case for the changes we desire, and building our power to make change. Women and men will work together in every industry, and company leaders will go beyond lip service and create real change, including equal pay and a zero-tolerance policy for sexual harassment. "Businesses will need to give women the tools to advance and both genders will have to recognize and wrangle with implicit biases in order to wring them out of the system," Feldt said.

POLITICS IS A JOB

Everywhere we see evidence of women's growing power and success. Having dedicated her career to building the collective political power of black women, Glynda Carr, founder of Higher Heights, believes that the government is no exception, and that it makes better decisions when the players at the table are diverse. Two-thirds of people surveyed in a 2014 Gallup poll said that America would be better off if more women held public office. All women, especially women of color, are still severely underrepresented and underserved. To remedy that, Carr urges women to open their minds to the bigger picture. For example, after the 2016 election the media focused almost exclusively on Hillary Clinton's loss (which was not for lack of trying by women of color). Yet Carr, speaking in the *YouTube* video "Beyond the Dream of 50/50," pointed out that black women had big wins that got barely a mention. They elected the largest number of women of color and the largest number of black women to Congress and state legislatures and sent the first black woman to Kentucky's legislature in twenty years. That's record-breaking success and abundance. "If we want to build economically stable communities, we must change the face of political leadership," she said, urging black women to run, vote, and take someone with them to the polls.

WOMEN USE THEIR "POWER TO" MAKE CHANGE

The number of women running for office in 2018 blew apart all previous records, and let's not forget that this is a sector of paid jobs that has long been off-limits for women. As reported by Charlotte Alter in *Time*, after the 2016 election more than twenty-six thousand women contacted Emily's List, which recruits and trains pro-choice Democratic women to run for office. The group knocked down a wall in its Washington office to make room for more staff. As of this writing, the number of Democratic women likely challenging incumbents in the US House of Representatives had tripled since 2016. At least seventy-seven women launched runs for governor in nearly every state in 2018, doubling a record set in 1994, according to the Center for American Women and Politics at Rutgers University.

Maggie's List reportedly also saw an increase in the number of conservative women running for office, although we were not able to find specific numbers. A federal political action committee, Maggie's List in February 2018 endorsed twelve women candidates they dubbed their Dynamic Dozen. For voters fed up with the two dominant parties, She Should Run, founded in 2011, billed itself as a nonpartisan organization offering support for women leaders considering a future run for office and for those who support them.

This year's female candidates are a diverse bunch, including immigrants, veterans, and an unprecedented number of women of color, who represent the fastest-growing voting bloc in the US. In fact, with more than 400 black women running as of this writing, as well as a surge in Latina, Asian American, and Native American candidates, 2018 could be the year that we finally shift the demographics of leadership. Kelly Dittmar, with the Center for American Women in Politics, sees that shift with a change in perception among the electorate, and women seeking office are finally being seen as qualified and capable. As Shirley Chisholm once said, "Our country needs women's idealism and determination, perhaps more in politics than anywhere else."

Even if we would never run for office, each of us can help move women toward equality in public policy jobs by volunteering for their campaigns and tapping into our assets to support their campaigns financially.

What Prompts Women's Aspirations?

Even though almost all women believe that it's harder for a woman to get elected than it is for a man, they are running anyway. That's great, because studies show that women actually win elections at the same rate as men, even though they are far less likely to run at all. According to Amanda Ripley, writing in *Politico*, women are less likely to be asked to run for elected office by a parent, friends, a teacher, a grandparent, or a coach than men are. Now that we know the strength of our unconscious biases against women's potential, we can consciously overcome them to support the aspirations of the women and girls around us.

It's important for women to understand that rising to fill a public policy job is not so different from rising to fill a corporate C-suite position. Both give us opportunities to exercise our "power to," whether by making laws to protect and support women, families, and communities or by creating jobs and helping other women advance at work.

ABUNDANCE, NOT SCARCITY

The doors of opportunity are indeed opening. "For the first time in 48 years of the World Economic Forum, held in Davos, Switzerland, 100 percent of the chairs of the summit were powerful women from across the globe," wrote Michele Weldon on Take The Lead's blog. These chairs included top leaders in unions, nuclear research, a global energy company, the International Monetary Fund, IBM Corporation, and microfinance banking, and the prime minister of Norway. Overall, women made up more than 21 percent of meeting attendees.

Canadian Prime Minister Justin Trudeau, an ardent supporter of women's equality, urged corporate leaders at Davos to consider gender-balancing their boards and project teams, reported Anna Bruce-Lockhart. "We need to be accountable for our efforts in an open and transparent way," Trudeau said. "In fact, we are in the process of passing legislation that would require federally incorporated companies to disclose information about their diversity policies. For example, this would include the proportion of women on their boards and senior management."

Sunshine laws like this and equal pay measures like Iceland's reflect the changing attitudes of our time. Two decades ago just twenty leaders in the modern world were women, according to the Council of Women World Leaders. Three years ago the membership of this exclusive council of women who had been elected president or prime minister had risen to fifty. Today, there are seventy female presidents and prime ministers—not enough, of course. But ask your friends how many top women leaders there are. You will learn, as Tiffany Shlain did when making her film *50/50: Rethinking the Past, Present & Future of Women + Power*, that women and men will guess a far smaller number. The story of scarcity that we have been telling for so long has blinded us to real progress in the modern world, Shlain said. No one wants to ally with a complainer or back a losing team. We need to tell a new, more accurate narrative of abundance that will help us get to a 50/50 world in which people of all genders share rights and responsibilities equally.

We need to tell a new, more accurate narrative of abundance that will help us get to a 50/50 world in which people of all genders share rights and responsibilities equally.

The Dalai Lama has predicted that women of the Western world will change the world for good. I believe we will, so I'm asking you to join together to support each other, and recruit allies to align with us as well.

PROGRESS AND PUSHBACK

Let's never forget the history of women's pursuit of equality, because that story helps us understand where we are today. Remember, for more than two hundred years, women have organized, fought, campaigned, sacrificed, and supported each other to gain the rights to inherit property, to keep their children, get an education, have a career, to vote, to hold office, and the list goes on. The women whose intersecting identities have marginalized them with less privilege nonetheless continue to lead our movement for women's equality. It's time to follow their lead. It's time to exercise those rights to achieve true equality now.

It's wonderful that we have experienced so much progress, but it's also troubling to encounter people who believe our problems have all been solved. Women with this attitude may undermine the ongoing efforts of their sisters to finish the job, perhaps as a way of avoiding conflict with the men in their lives. "Complete equality is not likely to occur if people fail to act because they believe that progress will take care of itself or that gender equality has already been fully achieved," Rudman and Glick noted. The biggest problem is, "These beliefs inhibit women from taking collective action, reducing the likelihood of future progress, and perhaps even threatening the erosion of gains that have already been made."

During the twentieth century women saw wins and losses, but the arc of history only bends toward justice *if we make it so*. Equality means equal in all things, so we're far from done. In fact, we're picking up the pace. Today, with the Internet, *Facebook*, *Twitter*, *Instagram*, and more, women have power and opportunity to spread their truths as never before.

GETTING TO INEVITABLE

Today, women are on their way to restoring an equitable balance of power in developed nations. To be sure, too many women around the world, including the most developed nations—like my home, the United States—still lack safety, opportunity, equality and well-being. We can keep the momentum going until everyone has risen, but only if we continue to work together. We need to support and reinforce each other's efforts. We need to elevate each other, one woman at a time.

> **"** There is no executive order; there is no law that can require the American people to form a national community. This we must do as individuals, and if we do it as individuals, there is no President of the United States who can veto that decision. **"**
>
> BARBARA JORDAN, civil rights leader, first African-American congresswoman from the Deep South, first woman elected to the Texas Senate

From a base of unique individuality, every woman around the world is a lot like you in fighting a hard battle for herself, her family, and her community. We need to reach out, stick together, and reinforce each other's efforts rather than turning our backs or undermining them.

SETTING UP A WOMEN'S GROUP

Paige Oxendine and Rachel Anderson learned that they shared a lot of common ground, so it was natural for them to start a women's group together, they said in an interview at their offices. Each had separately attended a weeklong policy workshop at the Sue Shear Institute for Women in Public Life in St. Louis. Each had experience lobbying, each had a powerful woman mentor, and each had run for and won the office of student body president at university. When their paths crossed as adults, they were united in a determination to make a difference and show what women could do. They recall the advice of mentor Vicky Riback Wilson, who served as Missouri state legislator from 1996 to 2004: "Do something every day that gets you out of your comfort zone. It's easy to play it safe and talk to the same five people at an event, but that doesn't create change."

> **❝I think change itself goes from the unthinkable, to the impossible, to the inevitable.❞**
>
> LAURA LISWOOD, secretary general of the Council of Women World Leaders, speaking in the film *50/50: Rethinking the Past, Present & Future of Women + Power*

Continuing their story in our interview, they said they noticed that the leadership of almost everything in their Springfield, Missouri, community could be characterized as overwhelmingly "male, pale, and stale," and they asked, "Where are all the young women and minorities?"

Contacts at the Missouri State University Foundation helped them apply for a grant from the Women's Foundation in Kansas City to set up a women's network, which they named Rosie. They orga-

nized a *Facebook* event, roughed out their website, RosieSGF
.com, and ordered some snacks for their launch party, hoping for fifty
attendees. By coincidence the launch party took place the week after
the November 2016 presidential election. More than 200 women
showed up, and they realized they had struck a nerve.

In the eighteen months that followed they worked to refine their
concept. Oxendine and Anderson were entirely intentional in forming Rosie, focusing on the specific needs they saw and drawing on
their established connections in
the community. Rosie is a no-cost
opportunity to meet other women,
learn of board service opportunities, and network for personal
development. It is not a lead-based
sales group. When people sign up online, their information popu-
lates a private database used to match people with opportunities such
as speaking, board service, or panels. Members can share information in a closed *Facebook* group. There are no monthly meetings, but
they said quarterly programs alternate between socials and learning
sessions, such as a recent Give It A Run program about how to seek
public office.

> **❝ The best thing to hold
> onto in life is each other.❞**
>
> AUDREY HEPBURN,
> actress

Early on they were surprised to notice men signing up on the
website, so they formed Brosie to capture the men's energy, now over
200 members strong. In their first year they marked Equal Pay Day
by launching the Rosie Makes Cents equal pay pledge. To date, more
than one hundred companies have signed the pledge and one large
business has conducted a wage audit. More than thirty-five women
have been placed on community boards, and Rosie continues to
share information about opportunities, encourage women to apply,
and follow up on applications with support.

The pair remind each other regularly to "do the one thing that you
can do," Oxendine said in concluding our interview. "The problems
in the world are so huge and burdensome, it's easy to become overwhelmed and think, 'There's no way I can make a dent.' But you can

make an introduction, leverage your social capital, bring someone along to an event, and make a tremendous difference in that person's life."

REWARDS OF CONNECTING

The best part of women connecting with women is that it's fun. It feeds your soul while you get things done. Women do this everywhere, drawing on the support of their peers united by a shared interest. In addition, everyone can mentor, sponsor, or support another woman, older, younger, above us or below us, in every industry and every country. Find those connections, foster them, and feel your joy and hope grow.

> Everyone can mentor, sponsor, or support another woman, older, younger, above us or below us, in every industry and every country.

In a blog post she wrote for Take The Lead about the film *A Wrinkle in Time*, Michele Weldon noted, "The underlying message for all women leaders embedded in this movie is very clear. An effective leader can be flawed, black, smart, young and female. And she can be mentored by amazing women who stick together and mine their own talents and flaws." Examples like this are helping to reverse the stereotypes that shut women out of influential roles, whether at home, in the community, on the job, or in our political capitols.

The positive energy is exciting, but Ms. Foundation for Women president and CEO Teresa C. Younger said in a *Biz Women* interview that what scares her the most about the year ahead is "that people will not be committed to staying uncomfortable in order to address these issues; that we will just react instead of planning and talking and figuring it out. In addition, the political atmosphere we're in is going to force us to think outside the box and play outside the rules.

We have become accustomed to playing inside the rules. We are paralyzing ourselves by playing within the rules, and we can't do that."

So, let's figure this out together. In a personal email in May 2018 social psychologist Peter Glick wrote to my team about resistance to women's advancement, saying, "The shock of a reasserted masculine power (replete with very explicit misogyny) seems to have jolted women into more activism and the realization that things are not going to take care of themselves without collective political and social action. But, prognosticating about where things go from here is a risky and uncertain business. The long-term view, I think, is still relatively sunny."

GETTING UNSTUCK

Let's not squander this opportunity. Clearly, this is our time, so let's keep the actions and momentum building. Let's ask for what we want, support other women in exercising our "power to," and believe in our abundant ability to change the world, together. Each small action can have a tremendous impact. Think of Frances McDormand's two words after she accepted her 2018 Oscar: "Inclusion rider." Most people had never heard these words before, but by saying just *two words*, McDormand prompted a national conversation about how a woman with a job can get more women hired. So simple.

PRACTICE JOY AND GRATITUDE

Meanwhile, let's never forget how fortunate we are to live in this time and be part of this movement for equality for all women, everywhere. We can dwell on what's wrong; we can worry if it will work. Or we can say, "Today is the first day of what remains of my life, and I want to see women achieve equality before I die." Which do you choose?

One woman supporting another woman: let's make that our daily practice. Gloria Allred said, "If each one of us made that sort of commitment to other women, to supporting other women, we would have social change very quickly." Imagine what the world will be like when each of us lives this way, wholeheartedly supporting other women. We will have equal pay, opportunity, advancement, health-care, safety, and so much more. I challenge you to find the one thing you can do *every day* to help another woman. No one else will do this for us, but we can do it for ourselves, because we are in this together.

SELECTED BIBLIOGRAPHY

Abouzahr, Katie, Jennifer Garcia-Alonso, Matt Krentz, Michael Tan, and Frances Brooks Taplett. "How Millennial Men Can Help Break the Glass Ceiling." Boston Consulting Group, November 1, 2017. www.bcg.com/en-us/publications/2017/people-organization-behavior-culture-how-millennial-men-can-help-break-glass-ceiling.aspx

Abouzahr, Katie, Matt Krentz, Frances Brooks Taplett, Claire Tracey, and Miki Tsusaka. "Dispelling the Myths of the Gender 'Ambition Gap.'" Boston Consulting Group, April 5, 2017. www.bcg.com/en-us/publications/2017/people-organization-leadership-change-dispelling-the-myths-of-the-gender-ambition-gap.aspx

Allred, Gloria, quoted in: Tolentino, Jia. "Gloria Allred's Crusade." *The New Yorker*, October 2, 2017. www.newyorker.com/magazine/2017/10/02/gloria-allreds-crusade

Alter, Charlotte. "A Year Ago, They Marched. Now a Record Number of Women Are Running for Office." *Time*, January 18, 2018. http://time.com/5107499/record-number-of-women-are-running-for-office

Alter, Charlotte. "Republicans Are Less Likely Than Democrats to Believe Women Who Make Sexual Assault Accusations: Survey." *Time*, December 6, 2017. http://time.com/5049665/republicans-democrats-believe-sexual-assault-accusations-survey

Anderson, Lisa. "Women Bosses Boost a Company's Bottom Line: Report." Thomson Reuters Foundation News, October 1, 2013. http://news.trust.org/item/20131001114303-nbevq

Aries, Emilie. "5 Ways Men Can Be Women's Allies at Work." *Forbes*, August 15, 2017. www.forbes.com/sites/emiliearies/2017/08/15/5-ways-men-can-be-womens-allies-at-work

Babcock, Linda, and Sara Laschever. *Women Don't Ask: Negotiation and the Gender Divide*. Princeton, NJ: Princeton University Press, 2003.

Barnett, Rosalind C., and Caryl Rivers. "How the 'New Discrimination' Is Holding Women Back." *Catalyst Blog*, April 17, 2014. www.catalyst.org/zing/how-new-discrimination-holding-women-back

Barnett, Rosalind C., and Caryl Rivers. *The New Soft War on Women: How the Myth of Female Ascendance Is Hurting Women, Men—and Our Economy.* New York: Jeremy P. Tarcher/Penguin, 2013.

BBC News. "California Drive-By Gunman Kills Six in Santa Barbara." *BBC News*, May 24, 2014. www.bbc.com/news/world-us-canada-27556097

Beal, Danna. *Healing the Workplace Culture.* Danna Beal. Accessed May 31, 2018. MP3 audio recording, 140 minutes. www.dannabeal.com/books-products

Biddle, Tabby. *Find Your Voice: A Woman's Call to Action.* Los Angeles: Women Press, 2015.

Blake, Emily. "How to Deal with Grown Up Mean Girls." *Filler*, April 13, 2012. http://fillermagazine.com/vida/love/how-to-deal-with-grown-up-mean-girls

Blanche, Aubrey, quoted in: Dishman, Lydia. "Women Leaders Share Moments of 2017 That Redefined Their Roles." *Fast Company*, December 13, 2017. www.fastcompany .com/40505186/women-leaders-share-moments-of-2017-that-redefined-their-roles

Bourgeois, Trudy. *Equality: Courageous Conversations About Women, Men, and Race to Spark a Diversity and Inclusion Breakthrough.* Charleston, SC: CreateSpace, 2017.

Bowles, Hannah Riley. "Why Women Don't Negotiate Their Job Offers." *Harvard Business Review*, June 19, 2014. https://hbr.org/2014/06/why-women-dont-negotiate-their-job-offers

Brands, Raina. "'Think Manager, Think Man' Stops Us Seeing Woman As Leaders." *The Guardian* (Manchester), July 15, 2015. www.theguardian.com/women-in-leadership/2015/jul/15/think-manager-think-man-women-leaders-biase-workplace

Bruce-Lockhart, Anna. "Justin Trudeau Tells Davos to Call Time on Women's Inequality." World Economic Forum, January 23, 2018. www.weforum.org/agenda/2018/01/justin-trudeau-davos-women-first

Budig, Michelle J. "The Fatherhood Bonus & the Motherhood Penalty." Third Way. Accessed April 27, 2018. http://content.thirdway.org/publications/853/NEXT_-_Fatherhood_Motherhood.pdf

Burke, Tarana, quoted in: Brockes, Emma. "Me Too Founder Tarana Burke: 'You Have to Use Your Privilege to Serve Other People.'" *The Guardian* (Manchester), January 15, 2018. www.theguardian.com/world/2018/jan/15/me-too-founder-tarana-burke-women-sexual-assault

Caprino, Kathy. "Gender Bias Is Real: Women's Perceived Competency Drops Significantly When Judged As Being Forceful." *Forbes*, August 25, 2015. www .forbes.com/sites/kathycaprino/2015/08/25/gender-bias-is-real-womens-perceived-competency-drops-significantly-when-judged-as-being-forceful

Center for American Women and Politics. "2018 Summary of Women Candidates." Rutgers University. Updated August 22, 2018. http://cawp.rutgers.edu/potential-candidate-summary-2018

Center for American Women and Politics. "History of Women of Color in US Politics." Rutgers University. Accessed July 15, 2018. www.cawp.rutgers.edu/history-women-color-us-politics

Center for American Women and Politics. "Women of Color in Elective Office 2018." Rutgers University. Accessed July 15, 2018. www.cawp.rutgers.edu/women-color-elective-office-2018

Center for Women and Business at Bentley University. "Men As Allies: Engaging Men to Advance Women in the Workplace." Spring 2017. www.ceoaction.com/media/1434/bentley-cwb-men-as-allies-research-report-spring-2017.pdf

Chemaly, Soraya. "How We Teach Our Kids That Women Are Liars." *Role Reboot*, November 19, 2013. www.rolereboot.org/culture-and-politics/details/2013-11-how-we-teach-our-kids-that-women-are-liars

Chesler, Phyllis. *Woman's Inhumanity to Woman*. New York: Nation Books, 2001.

Childress, Sarah. "Why the Military Has a Sexual Assault Problem." PBS *Frontline*, May 10, 2013. www.pbs.org/wgbh/frontline/article/why-the-military-has-a-rape-problem

Chism, Marlene. "The Hard Truth: Executive Conversation Is Not a Soft Skill." Marlene Chism, January 9, 2018. http://marlenechism.com/blog/the-hard-truth-executive-conversation-is-not-a-soft-skill

Chism, Marlene. *No-Drama Leadership*. New York: Routledge, 2016.

Chism, Marlene. *Stop Workplace Drama*. Hoboken, NJ: Wiley, 2011.

Chism, Marlene. "Workplace Conversations Drive Results or Drive Drama." Marlene Chism, February 20, 2018. http://marlenechism.com/blog/workplace-conversations-drive-results-or-drive-drama

Choi, Grace. "What We Learned about Sexual Harassment after 100+ Hours of Interviews." *Medium*, July 10, 2017. https://medium.com/betterbrave/https-medium-com-g-choi-what-we-learned-about-sexual-harassment-after-100-hours-of-interviews-7dfbf22b6777

Christakis, Erika. "Why Are Women Biased Against Other Women?" *Time*, October 4, 2012. http://ideas.time.com/2012/10/04/womens-inhumanity-to-women

Clivilez-Wu, Isabella. "The Top Three Workplace Challenges for Millennials." *Forbes*, April 28, 2016. www.forbes.com/sites/under30network/2016/04/28/the-top-three-workplace-challenges-for-millennials

Crenshaw, Kimberlé. "Why Intersectionality Can't Wait." *The Washington Post*, September 24, 2015. www.washingtonpost.com/news/in-theory/wp/2015/09/24/ why-intersectionality-cant-wait/?utm_term=.81999a97eb4c

Crowley, Katherine, quoted in: Smith, Jacquelyn. "How to Deal with Cliques at Work." *Forbes*, July 25, 2013. www.forbes.com/sites/jacquelynsmith/2013/07/25/ how-to-deal-with-cliques-at-work

Development Dimensions International. "Ready-Now Leaders: 25 Findings to Meet Tomorrow's Business Challenges: Global Leadership Forecast 2014-2015." www .ddiworld.com/DDI/media/trend-research/global-leadership-forecast-2014-2015_tr_ ddi.pdf

Devlin, Hannah. "Early Men and Women Were Equal, Say Scientists." *The Guardian* (Manchester), May 14, 2015. www.theguardian.com/science/2015/may/14/early-men-women-equal-scientists

Dizikes, Peter. "Study: Workplace Diversity Can Help the Bottom Line." *MIT News*, October 7, 2014. http://news.mit.edu/2014/workplace-diversity-can-help-bottom-line-1007

Dobbin, Frank, and Alexandra Kalev. "Why Diversity Programs Fail." *Harvard Business Review*, July-August 2016. https://hbr.org/2016/07/why-diversity-programs-fail

Dodgson, Lindsay. "The Biggest Excuses Narcissists Spin to Keep You Hooked— and Why This Makes Them Dangerous." *Business Insider*, December 9, 2017. www .businessinsider.com/the-biggest-excuses-narcissists-spin-to-keep-you-hooked-2017-12

Dufu, Tiffany. *Drop the Ball: Achieving More by Doing Less*. New York: Flatiron Books, 2017.

Ellingrud, Kweilin, Anu Madgavkar, James Manyika, Jonathan Woetzel, Vivian Riefberg, Mekala Krishnan, and Mili Seoni. "The Power of Parity: Advancing Women's Equality in the United States." McKinsey Global Institute, April 2016. www.mckinsey.com/global-themes/employment-and-growth/the-power-of-parity-advancing-womens-equality-in-the-united-states

Equal Pay Today! "Equal Pay Day." Accessed May 16, 2018. www.equalpaytoday.org/ equalpaydays

Fairygodboss. "Want to Support Your Female Coworkers, Men? Start by Doing These 5 Things." Accessed May 9, 2018. https://fairygodboss.com/articles/jobs/ want-to-support-your-female-coworkers-men-start-by-doing-these-5-things

Feldt, Gloria. "How Companies Must Adapt in the #MeToo Era." *Time*, January 29, 2018. http://time.com/5120607/companies-leadership-metoo-era

Feldt, Gloria. *No Excuses: 9 Ways Women Can Change How We Think About Power*. Berkeley, CA: Seal Press, 2010.

Feldt, Gloria, quoted in: Weldon, Michele. "Google This: Best Ways to Handle a Hostile Coworker Who Shows Gender Bias." *Take The Lead The Movement Blog*, August 11, 2017. www.taketheleadwomen.com/blog/google-this-best-ways-to-handle-a-hostile-coworker-who-shows-gender-bias

Fisher-Blando, Judith Lynn. "Workplace Bullying: Aggressive Behavior and Its Effect on Job Satisfaction and Productivity." PhD diss., University of Phoenix, 2008. www.workplaceviolence911.com/docs/20081215.pdf

Fizer, Ashten, quoted in: Blavity Team. "What Being a Unicorn Really Means and How to Channel Positivity in Your Career." *Blavity*. Accessed May 24, 2018. https://blavity.com/what-being-a-unicorn-really-means-and-how-to-channel-positivity-in-your-career

Fortune Editors. "These Are the Women CEOs Leading *Fortune* 500 Companies." *Fortune*, June 7, 2017. http://fortune.com/2017/06/07/fortune-500-women-ceos

Frostenson, Sarah. "More Women Are Running, But Will They Win?" *Politico*. Updated May 16, 2018. www.politico.com/interactives/2018/women-rule-candidate-tracker

Gabriel, Allison S., Marcus M. Butts, Zhenyu Yuan, Rebecca L. Rosen, and Michael T. Sliter. "Further Understanding Incivility in the Workplace: The Effects of Gender, Agency, and Communion." *Journal of Applied Psychology* 103, no. 4 (2018): 362–382. http://psycnet.apa.org/record/2017-56107-001

Gabriel, Allison, quoted in: Ang, Katerina. "Why Women Are Meaner to Each Other Than Men Are to Women." *Moneyish*, March 4, 2018. https://moneyish.com/ish/why-women-are-meaner-to-each-other-than-men-are-to-women

Garamone, Jim. "Independent Survey Shows Decline in Military Sexual Assaults." US Department of Defense, May 1, 2015. www.defense.gov/News/Article/Article/604560

Garcia-Alonso, Jennifer, Matt Krentz, Frances Brooks Taplett, Claire Tracey, and Miki Tsusaka. "Getting the Most from Your Diversity Dollars." Boston Consulting Group, June 21, 2017. www.bcg.com/en-us/publications/2017/people-organization-behavior-culture-getting-the-most-from-diversity-dollars.aspx

Ghosn, Caroline, quoted in: Gallagher, Molly. "5 Ways to Ooze Confidence—and Professionalism—on the Job." *Well+Good*, March 15, 2015. www.wellandgood.com/good-advice/5-ways-to-ooze-confidence-and-professionalism-on-the-job

Gillis, Deborah. "The Politics of Women in Leadership." *Catalyst Blog*, October 25, 2016. www.catalyst.org/blog/catalyzing/politics-women-leadership

Giscombe, Katherine. "Sexual Harassment and Women of Color." *Catalyst Blog*, February 13, 2018. www.catalyst.org/blog/catalyzing/sexual-harassment-and-women-color

Glaser, Tanya. "Summary of 'Constructive Confrontation: A Transformative Approach to Intractable Conflicts.'" *Beyond Intractability.* Accessed May 17, 2018. www.beyondintractability.org/artsum/burgess-confrontation

Glick, Peter, and Susan T. Fiske. "Ambivalent Sexism." *Advances in Experimental Social Psychology* Vol. 33 (2001), edited by Mark P. Zanna, 115–188. Thousand Oaks, CA: Academic Press. www.sciencedirect.com/science/article/pii/S0065260101800058

Grossman, Roberta, and Sophie Sartain. *Seeing Allred.* Netflix, 2018. www.netflix.com/search?q=seeing a&jbv=80174367&jbp=0&jbr=0

Gupta, Shalene. "Study: 100% of Women of Color in STEM Experience Bias." *Fortune,* January 26, 2015. http://fortune.com/2015/01/26/study-100-of-women-of-color-in-stem-experience-bias

Guys Who Get It Awards. January 26, 2017. www.guyswhogetitawards.com

Hardy, Anne, quoted in: *Knowledge@Wharton.* "'Masculine Norms': Why Working Women Find It Hard to Reach the Top." *Knowledge@Wharton,* August 3, 2011. http://knowledge.wharton.upenn.edu/article/masculine-norms-why-working-women-find-it-hard-to-reach-the-top

Harris, Carla. "How to Own Your Power Presentation." *YouTube,* 20:46. February 19, 2014. www.youtube.com/watch?v=0rWmtyZXkFg&feature=youtu.be

Hartley, Gemma. "Women Aren't Nags—We're Just Fed Up." *Harper's Bazaar,* September 27, 2017. www.harpersbazaar.com/culture/features/a12063822/emotional-labor-gender-equality/?linkId=42945124

Hay, Louise. "Job Success." Louise Hay. Accessed May 26, 2018. www.louisehay.com/job-success

Hayek, Salma, quoted in: Vourlias, Christopher. "Salma Hayek on the Cannes Women's Protest and the Downfall of Harvey Weinstein." *Variety,* May 13, 2018. http://variety.com/2018/film/news/salma-hayek-harvey-weinstein-cannes-women-in-motion-1202808768

Hegewisch, Ariane, and Emma Williams-Baron. "The Gender Wage Gap: 2017 Earnings Differences by Race and Ethnicity." Institute for Women's Policy Research, March 7, 2018. https://iwpr.org/publications/gender-wage-gap-2017-race-ethnicity

Hoberman, Judy. *Walking on the Glass Floor: Seven Essential Qualities of Women Who Lead.* Southlake, TX: Walking on the Glass Floor Press, 2018.

Hoffman, Gene Knudsen, Cynthia Monroe, and Leah Green. "Compassionate Listening: An Exploratory Sourcebook about Conflict Transformation." New Conversations Initiative, March 2012. https://newconversations.net/pdf/compassionate_listening.pdf

Hopkins, Anne (lawsuit). Price Waterhouse v. Hopkins, 490 U.S. 228, 87-1167 (Supreme Court of the United States 31 October 1988).

Hunt, Vivian, Dennis Layton, and Sara Prince. "Diversity Matters." McKinsey & Company, February 2, 2015. www.mckinsey.com/business-functions/organization/our-insights/why-diversity-matters

Hunt, Vivian, Sara Prince, Sundiatu Dixon-Fyle, and Lareina Yee. "Delivering Through Diversity." McKinsey & Company, January 2018. www.mckinsey.com/~/media/mckinsey/business functions/organization/our insights/delivering through diversity/delivering-through-diversity_full-report.ashx

Hyde, Janet Shibley. "The Gender Similarities Hypothesis." *American Psychologist* 60, no. 6 (September 2005): 581–592. www.apa.org/pubs/journals/releases/amp-606581.pdf

Inspirations for Youth and Families. "How to Help Your Child Survive and Overcome Teen Bullying." Inspirations for Youth and Families, August 29, 2017. https://inspirationsyouth.com/how-to-help-your-child-survive-and-overcome-teen-bullying

Jackson, Robert Max. *Destined for Equality: The Inevitable Rise of Women's Status.* Cambridge, MA: Harvard University Press, 1998.

Jamieson, Dave. "'He Was Masturbating...I Felt Like Crying': What Housekeepers Endure to Clean Hotel Rooms." *HuffPost*, November 18, 2017. www.huffingtonpost.com/entry/housekeeper-hotel-sexual-harassment_us_5a0f438ce4b0e97dffed3443

Joy, Lois, Nancy M. Carter, Harvey M. Wagner, and Sriram Narayanan. "The Bottom Line: Corporate Performance and Women's Representation On Boards." Catalyst, October 15, 2007. www.catalyst.org/knowledge/bottom-line-corporate-performance-and-womens-representation-boards

Kamps, Louisa. "6 Surprising Reasons Why Gratitude Is Great for Your Health." *Real Simple.* Accessed May 5, 2018. www.realsimple.com/health/mind-mood/why-gratitude-is-great-for-your-health

Katz, Jackson, quoted in: Plank, Liz. "Most Perpetrators of Sexual Violence Are Men, So Why Do We Call It a Women's Issue?" Divided States of Women, November 2, 2017. www.dividedstatesofwomen.com/2017/11/2/16597768/sexual-assault-men-himthough

Keller, Jared. "The Rise and Fall (and Rise) of 'Marines United.'" *Task & Purpose*, March 16, 2017. https://taskandpurpose.com/rise-fall-rise-marines-united

Kessler, Glenn. "Do 10,000 Baby Boomers Retire Every Day?" *The Washington Post*, July 24, 2014. www.washingtonpost.com/news/fact-checker/wp/2014/07/24/do-10000-baby-boomers-retire-every-day/?utm_term=.af19699ff07a

Kimmel, Michael. "Why Gender Equality Is Good for Everyone—Men Included." Filmed May 2015 in Monterey, CA. TEDWomen Video, 15:59. www.ted.com/talks/michael_kimmel_why_gender_equality_is_good_for_everyone_men_included

King, Martin Luther Jr. Interview by Sander Vancour. *NBC News*. Video File. May 8, 1967. www.nbcnews.com/video/martin-luther-king-jr-speaks-with-nbc-news-11-months-before-assassination-1202163779741?cid=sm_npd_nn_tw_ma

Kingsolver, Barbara. "#MeToo Isn't Enough. Now Women Need to Get Ugly." *The Guardian* (Manchester), January 16, 2018. www.theguardian.com/commentisfree/2018/jan/16/metoo-women-daughters-harassment-powerful-men

Knowles-Carter, Beyoncé. "Gender Equality Is a Myth!" The Shriver Report, January 12, 2014. http://shriverreport.org/gender-equality-is-a-myth-beyonce

Kratz, Julie. *ONE: How Male Allies Support Women for Gender Equality.* Indianapolis, IN: Niche Pressworks, 2017.

Krawcheck, Sallie. *Own It: The Power of Women at Work.* New York: Crown Business, 2017.

Kreisinger, Elisa. "What's the Deal with White Men?" Strong Opinions Loosely Held/RIOT. *YouTube*, 4:58. Posted August 11, 2018. www.youtube.com/watch?v=mWFwrYnRiE4&t=217s

Kristof, Nicholas. "Steinem, Sandberg and Judd on How to End Sex Harassment." *The New York Times*, October 25, 2017. www.nytimes.com/2017/10/25/opinion/sexual-harassment-men.html

Krook, Anne. "How Men Can Help." Anne Krook: Practical Workplace Advice. Accessed May 20, 2018. http://annekrook.com/?page_id=1230

Krook, Anne. *Now What Do I Say? Practical Workplace Advice for Younger Women.* Amazon Digital Services, 2014.

Langer, Gary. "Unwanted Sexual Advances Not Just a Hollywood, Weinstein Story, Poll Finds." *ABC News*, October 17, 2017. http://abcnews.go.com/Politics/unwanted-sexual-advances-hollywood-weinstein-story-poll/story?id=50521721

Lartey, Jamiles, and Joanna Walters. "Women Dominate Congressional Primaries—Now to Win Office." *The Guardian* (Manchester), May 12, 2018. www.theguardian.com/us-news/2018/may/12/the-resistance-now-women-congressional-primaries-midterms-2018

Lawrence, Jennifer. "Why Do I Make Less Than My Male Co-stars?" *Lenny Letter,* October 13, 2015. www.lennyletter.com/story/jennifer-lawrence-why-do-i-make-less-than-my-male-costars

LeanIn.org and McKinsey & Company. *Women in the Workplace 2017.* Accessed April 27, 2018. https://womenintheworkplace.com/Women_in_the_Workplace_2017.pdf

Lee, Loretta, quoted in: Wong, Julia Carrie. "Google's 'Bro-Culture' Meant Routine Sexual Harassment of Women, Suit Says." *The Guardian* (Manchester), February 28, 2018. www.theguardian.com/technology/2018/feb/28/google-lawsuit-sexual-harassment-bro-culture?

LeMay, Kathy. "Listen: My Five Takeaways from a Year of Listening." Kathy LeMay, December 20, 2017. www.kathy-lemay.com/single-post/2017/12/20/Listen-My-Five-Takeaways-From-a-Year-of-Listening

Lucas, Jackson. "Protecting Low-Wage Workers and Women of Color." Rave Mobile Safety, January 10, 2018. www.ravemobilesafety.com/blog/protecting-low-wage-workers-and-women-of-color

Mandavilli, Apoorva. "Calculating a Gender Bias in Neuroscience." *Post and Courier* (Charleston), September 11, 2016. www.postandcourier.com/health/calculating-a-gender-bias-in-neuroscience/article_04ce3bdc-8b6a-5cc5-b943-0bb9373f2bf5.html

Mansbridge, Jane, quoted in: Loewi, Ethan G. "Painting a New Path at the Kennedy School." *Harvard Crimson*, March 5, 2012. www.thecrimson.com/article/2012/3/5/women-portraits-kennedy-school

Marcos, Cristina. "115th Congress Will Be Most Racially Diverse in History." *The Hill*, November 17, 2016. http://thehill.com/homenews/house/306480-115th-congress-will-be-most-racially-diverse-in-history

Milne-Tyte, Ashley. "Why Women Don't Ask for More Money." NPR's *Planet Money*, April 8, 2014. www.npr.org/sections/money/2014/04/08/300290240/why-women-dont-ask-for-more-money

Moore, Jack. "Women Vets Have More Than Double the Suicide Rate of Civilian Women." *Newsweek*, September 21, 2017. www.newsweek.com/women-vets-have-more-double-suicide-rate-civilian-women-668732

Namie, Gary, quoted in: Carpenter, Julia. "What to Do When Your Boss Is a Bully." CNN, January 15, 2018. http://money.cnn.com/2018/01/15/pf/bosses-work-bullying/index.html

Namie, Gary, quoted in: Cheek, Tessa. "Mean Girls, All Grown Up, Now Workplace Bullies." *Colorado Independent*, September 24, 2013. www.coloradoindependent.com/144111/mean-girls-all-grown-up-now-workplace-bullies

Nelson, Sophia A. "Sophia A. Nelson, Esq." *Women Change the World: Noteworthy Women on Cultivating Your Potential and Achieving Success*, edited by Michelle Patterson, 87–88. Dallas, TX: BenBella Books, 2014.

Newsom, Jennifer Siebel. *The Mask You Live In*. Netflix, 2015. www.netflix.com/title/80076159

Newsom, Jennifer Siebel. "2017: Silent No Longer." *HuffPost*, November 30, 2017. www.huffingtonpost.com/entry/2017-silent-no-longer_us_5a202959e4b02edd56c6d75c

Noland, Marcus, Tyler Moran, and Barbara Kotschwar. "Is Gender Diversity Profitable? Evidence from a Global Survey." Peterson Institute for International Economics Working Paper. WP 16-3, February 2016. https://piie.com/publications/wp/wp16-3.pdf

O'Reilly, Nancy D. *Leading Women: 20 Influential Women Share Their Secrets to Leadership, Business, and Life*. Avon, MA: Adams Media, 2014.

Ong, Thuy. "Wonder Woman 2 Will Be the First Production to Adopt New Anti-Sexual Harassment Guidelines." *The Verge*, January 22, 2018. www.theverge.com/2018/1/22/16918368/wonder-woman-2-producers-guild-america-pga-anti-sexual-harassment-guidelines

Oswald, Andrew. "New Study Suggests Women Do Ask for Pay Raises but Don't Get Them." University of Warwick, Department of Economics, September 5, 2016. https://warwick.ac.uk/fac/soc/economics/news/2016/9/new_study_suggests_women_do_ask_for_pay_rises_but_dont_get_them

Parker, Kim. "Women in Majority-Male Workplaces Report Higher Rates of Gender Discrimination." Pew Research Center, March 7, 2018. www.pewresearch.org/fact-tank/2018/03/07/women-in-majority-male-workplaces-report-higher-rates-of-gender-discrimination

Pascal, Amy, quoted in: Berman, Eliza. "How Greta Gerwig Is Leading By Example." *Time*, March 1, 2018. http://time.com/magazine/us/5180696/march-12th-2018-vol-191-no-10-u-s

Peluso, Michelle. "IBM's CMO Michelle Peluso on Recruiting Women Who Left Work Years Ago." Women 2.0, March 12, 2018. www.women2.com/2018/03/12/ibms-cmo-michelle-peluso-on-recruiting-women-who-left-work-years-ago

"Pregnancy Risk Puts Employers Off Women." *Scotsman* (Edinburgh, Scotland), April 20, 2008. www.scotsman.com/news/pregnancy-risk-puts-employers-off-women-1-1164269

Raisman, Aly, quoted in: Graves, Will. "Olympic Star Raisman Files Suit Against USOC, USA Gymnastics." *Salt Lake Tribune*, March 2, 2018. www.sltrib.com/sports/2018/03/02/olympic-star-raisman-files-suit-against-usoc-usa-gymnastics

Rattigan, Kaitlin. "Why Am I Deciding to Thrive and Lean In? Because Confidence Matters." *Take The Lead The Movement Blog*, April 28, 2014. www.taketheleadwomen.com/blog/deciding-thrive-lean-confidence-matters

Reardon, Kathleen Kelley. "Getting Past Stereotypes That Limit Women's Power." Big Think Edge. Accessed April 27, 2018. http://bigthink.com/influence-power-politics/getting-past-stereotypes-that-limit-womens-power

Rendleman, Linda. "Some Women Don't Get It." Linda Rendleman, February 16, 2016. www.lindarendleman.com/2016/02/16/some-women-dont-get-it

Ripley, Amanda. "What It Will Take for Women to Win." *Politico*, June 12, 2017. www.politico.com/interactives/2017/women-rule-politics

Rivers, Dennis. *The Seven Challenges Workbook, 9th ed.* New Conversations Initiative, 2015. https://newconversations.net/sevenchallenges.pdf

Robinson, Sheila A. *Lead by Example: An Insider's Look at How to Successfully Lead in Corporate America and Entrepreneurship.* Burlington, NC: Diversity Woman Media, LLC, 2014.

Rock, Maxine. "Reputation Alert." *Pink*, April/May, 2007.

Rodin, Dr. Judith, and Monique Villa. "Want to Boost Women's Careers? Raise Their Expectations." *HuffPost*, October 13, 2016. www.huffingtonpost.com/judith-rodin/want-to-boost-womens-careers_b_8286122.html

Rudman, Laurie A., and Peter Glick. *The Social Psychology of Gender: How Power and Intimacy Shape Gender Relations.* New York: Guilford Press, 2008.

Salazar, Janet C. "Janet Salazar." *Women Change the World*, edited by Michelle Patterson, 176–180. Dallas, TX: BenBella Books, 2014.

Sanbonmatsu, Kira, Susan J. Carroll, and Debbie Walsh. *Poised to Run.* New Brunswick, NJ: Center for American Women and Politics (CAWP), Eagleton Institute of Politics, Rutgers, The State University of New Jersey, 2009. www.cawp.rutgers.edu/sites/default/files/resources/poisedtorun_0.pdf

Sandberg, Sheryl. "Facebook COO Sheryl Sandberg's Top Five Ways for Women to Support Women." *People*, November 2, 2016. http://people.com/human-interest/facebook-coo-sheryl-sandbergs-top-five-ways-for-women-to-support-women

Schmidt, Samantha. "New Zealand's Prime Minister Is Pregnant: 'I Am Not the First Woman to Multitask,' She Says." *The Washington Post*, January 19, 2018. www.washingtonpost.com/news/morning-mix/wp/2018/01/19/new-zealands-prime-minister-is-pregnant-i-am-not-the-first-woman-to-multitask-she-says/?noredirect=on&utm_term=.dcb86f7b8ac8

Seabrook, Linda A. "The Top 10 Things Employers Can Do Right Now to Address Sexual Harassment in the Workplace." Futures Without Violence, November 2, 2017. www.futureswithoutviolence.org/employers-sexual-harassment

Shelton, Chuck. "Eight Ways to Engage Men as Allies (and Two to Avoid)." Diversity Best Practices, November 10, 2014. www.diversitybestpractices.com/blogs/post/eight-ways-engage-men-allies-and-two-avoid

Shlain, Tiffany. *50/50: Rethinking the Past, Present & Future of Women + Power.* Let It Ripple Film Studio, 2016. www.letitripple.org/films/50-50

Shook, Ellyn, and Julie Sweet. "Getting to Equal 2018: Creating a Culture Where Everyone Thrives." Accenture. Accessed May 26, 2018. www.accenture.com/t20180307T184141Z__w__/us-en/_acnmedia/PDF-73/Accenture-When-She-Rises-We-All-Rise.pdf

Shorey, Missy. "Maggie's List, a Leading Federal PAC for Conservative Women, Endorses the 'Dynamic Dozen' with More to Come in the 2018 Primary Election Cycle." PRWeb, August 23, 2018. www.prweb.com/releases/2018/02/prweb15179747.htm

Sinema, Kyrsten, quoted in: Sanders, Rebekah L. "The Congresswoman Who Grew Up in a Gas Station." *AZ Central* (Phoenix). Accessed May 24, 2018. www.azcentral.com/story/news/arizona/politics/2016/01/30/congresswoman-who-grew-up-gas-station/79206952

Small, Meredith F. "The Evolution of Bullying." *LiveScience*, October 12, 2007. www.livescience.com/1947-evolution-bullying.html

Snyder, Kieran. "The Abrasiveness Trap: High-Achieving Men and Women Are Described Differently in Reviews." *Fortune*, August 26, 2014. http://fortune.com/2014/08/26/performance-review-gender-bias

Sobel, Ariel. "Average LGBT Student Carries $16K More Debt Than Straight Peers." *The Advocate*, July 23, 2018. www.advocate.com/business/2018/7/23/average-lgbtq-student-carries-16k-more-debt-straight-peers

State of California Department of Industrial Relations. "California Equal Pay Act," October 2017. www.dir.ca.gov/dlse/California_Equal_Pay_Act.htm

Take The Lead Women. "Beyond the Dream of 50/50—Virtual Happy Hour." *YouTube*, 1:03:08. Posted April 18, 2018. www.youtube.com/watch?v=JcZO2YDvcX8

Taylor, Shelley E., Laura Cousino Klein, Brian P. Lewis, Tara L. Gruenewald, Regan A.R. Gurung, and John A. Updegraff. "Behavioral Responses to Stress in Females: Tend-and-Befriend, Not Fight-or-Flight." *Psychological Review* 107, no. 3 (May 2000): 411–429. https://taylorlab.psych.ucla.edu/wp-content/uploads/sites/5/2014/10/2000_Biobehavioral-responses-to-stress-in-females_tend-and-befriend.pdf

Tchen, Tina, quoted in: Eckardt, Stephanie. "What's Next for Time's Up According to Tina Tchen, the Powerhouse Lawyer Behind the Famous Faces." *W*, January 8, 2018. www.wmagazine.com/story/times-up-legal-defense-fund-tina-tchen-interview

Tchen, Tina, quoted in Calkins, Kelley. "An Interview with Michelle Obama's Chief of Staff, Tina Tchen." *HuffPost*, updated February 8, 2017. www.huffingtonpost.com/kelley-calkins/michelle-obama-chief-of-s_b_9177542.html

Thomas, Gillian, quoted in: Connley, Courtney. "5 Things Men Can Do Right Now to Support Women at Work." CNBC, December 22, 2017. www.cnbc.com/2017/12/21/5-things-men-can-do-right-now-to-support-women-at-work.html

Tuttle, Kate. "Why We Don't Believe What Women Say." *The Boston Globe*, January 13, 2017. www.bostonglobe.com/arts/books/2017/01/12/why-don-believe-what-women-say/bktOcaTkRlXuhOd3VQf1hK/story.html

Wakeman, Cy. "Overcoming 'Us vs. Them' Challenges." *Fast Company*, January 23, 2014. www.fastcompany.com/3025378/overcoming-us-vs-them-challenges

Weber, Lauren. "Why Young Women Play Down Their Career Goals Around Men." *The Wall Street Journal*, January 24, 2017. www.wsj.com/articles/young-single-women-try-to-appear-less-ambitious-to-attract-a-mate-study-1485270001

Weida, Kaz. "Why Conservative Women Vote for Alleged Sexual Abusers." *Rantt Media*, December 8, 2017. https://rantt.com/why-women-vote-for-sexual-predators

Weldon, Michele. "The Promise of Davos: World Economic Forum Shines on Women's Leadership." *Take The Lead The Movement Blog*, January 29, 2018. www.taketheleadwomen.com/blog/the-promise-of-davos-world-economic-forum-shines-on-womens-leadership

Wells, Georgia. "Stanford Announces 'Bootcamp' for Gay Business Leaders." *The Wall Street Journal*, January 6, 2016. www.wsj.com/articles/stanford-announces-bootcamp-for-gay-business-leaders-1452102442

Williams, John E., and Deborah L. Best. *Measuring Sex Stereotypes: A Multination Study* (rev. ed.). Newbury Park, CA: Sage, 1990.

Williams, Joan C., and Rachel Dempsey. *What Works for Women at Work: Four Patterns Working Women Need to Know*. New York: New York University Press, 2014.

Wilson, Jamia. Interview by Senti Sojwal. "The Feministing Five: Jamia Wilson." *Feministing*. Accessed May 16, 2018. http://feministing.com/2017/10/04/the-feministing-five-jamia-wilson

Yong, Ed. "15-Minute Writing Exercise Closes the Gender Gap in University-Level Physics." *Discover*, November 25, 2010. http://blogs.discovermagazine.com/notrocketscience/2010/11/25/15-minute-writing-exercise-closes-the-gender-gap-in-university-level-physics

YW Boston. "What Is Intersectionality, and What Does It Have to Do with Me?" *YW Boston Blog*, March 29, 2017. www.ywboston.org/2017/03/what-is-intersectionality-and-what-does-it-have-to-do-with-me

Zalis, Shelley. "The New Rules of Feminism." *Forbes*, June 5, 2017. www.forbes.com/sites/shelleyzalis/2017/06/05/why-the-new-wave-of-femenism-must-include-men-and-how-to-get-there

Zarya, Valentina. "Men Told Hillary Clinton to 'Smile' During Her DNC Speech." *Fortune*, July 29, 2016. http://fortune.com/2016/07/29/men-hillary-clinton-smile

Zarya, Valentina. "Share of Female CEOs in the *Fortune* 500 Dropped by 25% in 2018." *Fortune*, May 21, 2018. http://fortune.com/2018/05/21/women-fortune-500-2018/

Zook, Kristal B. *Black Women's Lives: Stories of Power and Pain*. New York: Nation Books, 2006.

Zook, Kristal B. *I See Black People: The Rise and Fall of African American–Owned Television and Radio*. New York: Nation Books, 2008.

INDEX

Rivers, Dennis, 214
Robinson, Sheila, 33, 39, 62, 69, 129, 134, 158–59, 169, 220
Rock, Maxine, 146
Rodger, Elliot, 180–81
Rodin, Judith, 168
Roediger, Ant, 203
Roem, Danica, 188
Rowling, J.K., 173
Roys, Kelda, 81
Rudman, Laurie A., 49, 51–54, 57, 67, 84, 190, 193, 229

Salazar, Janet C., 218
Sanbonmatsu, Kira, 36
Sandberg, Sheryl, 77
Sartain, Sophie, 188
Schaeffer, Ellen, 55–56
Schlafly, Phyllis, 131
Schmidt, Samantha, 81
Seabrook, Linda, 206
"Second shift" burden, 52–54
Self-doubt, overcoming, 28, 97–99
Self-worth, 22, 46, 79, 82–83, 89–91, 125, 168
Sexism
    ambivalent sexism, 47–48, 174, 205
    benevolent sexism, 48
    Goldilocks syndrome, 50–52
    hostile sexism, 49
    internalized sexism, 50
    "second shift" burden, 52–54
    types of, 47–54
Sexual bias, 62–63
Sexual discrimination, 186. See also Discrimination
Sexual harassment. See Harassment
Sexual orientations, 19, 32, 58, 62–63, 92, 107, 142–43
Sharpnack, Rayona, 220
Shlain, Tiffany, 54–55, 90, 228

Shook, Ellyn, 31
Sinema, Kyrsten, 188
Small, Meredith, 130
Smith, Jacquelyn, 135
Snyder, Kieran, 79
Social changes, 27–28, 56–59, 223–34
Social media, using, 26, 56, 67, 82, 142, 160, 205–8, 229–31
Social pressure, 45, 56–59
Sojwal, Senti, 65
Sreenivasan, Hari, 184
STEM careers, 55–56, 63–64
Stereotypes. See Gender stereotypes
StopSexism Social Interest Group, 178
Strengths
    for advancement, 18–19, 21–117
    leadership and, 25–28, 84
    power and, 17–19, 25–28
    strong characteristics, 70–73
    of women, 18–19, 21–117
Success
    balanced leadership for, 38–39, 86–88
    challenges for, 83
    equal leadership and, 38–39, 86–88
    focus on, 25
    leadership and, 38–40
    opportunities for, 18, 22–32, 89–117, 227–34
    room for achieving, 89
    sharing, 82–83, 89
    team success, 89
Summers, Lawrence, 67
Support for women, 17–18, 23–40, 72–76, 85–117, 137–70, 193–204, 223–34
Support groups, 40, 98
Sweet, Julie, 31

Tallon, Monique, 39
Tan, Michael, 203